Retire on Rails of Steel

Michael R. Panico, CFP®

Arcadia Financial Group, LLC
SALEM, NEW HAMPSHIRE

Michael R. Panico, CFP®/Arcadia Financial Group, LLC
44 Stiles Rd., Suite 2
Salem, NH 03079
https://arcadia.financial

Book layout ©2013 BookDesignTemplates.com

Retire on Rails of Steel/ Michael R. Panico, CFP®. —1st ed.
ISBN 978-1979770163

Contents

Dedicated to my wife and best friend, Jessica, who nurtures everything good in my life. Make way!

INTRODUCTION

*"We hold these truths to be self-evident, that all men are created equal,
that they are endowed by their Creator with certain unalienable Rights,
that among these are Life, Liberty and the pursuit of Happiness."*
— Thomas Jefferson,
the Declaration of Independence

History is nuanced and complicated beyond telling, but it wouldn't
be much of a stretch to say that retirement would not be possible
if not for the penning of those words.

The American experiment would make its mark on history by
breaking men from the bonds of tyranny so they might be sovereign
only to principles grounded in freedom. A person's success could
then be defined not by station or birthright, but by the fruits of their
own labor and effort.

Americans wasted no time in using this newfound freedom to
blaze a trail of innovation that would propel humanity forward at
breakneck speed. The path has not been straightforward, marred by
our struggle to treat each other peaceably and with respect, but such

is the rhythm of history. Our failings serve as lessons so future generations can forge a better path.

The American march toward prosperity is perhaps best exemplified by the transformative effect of the transcontinental railroad system. With a vast expanse of unoccupied territory, growing population and entrepreneurial spirit, Americans viewed the steam locomotive as a key to fulfilling Manifest Destiny—the belief that our country should span the continent from sea to shining sea.

The railroads accelerated westward expansion and created a paradigm shift in economic efficiency. For the first time in history, natural resources and agricultural output could speed across hundreds of miles to city centers, ports and markets. Goods, people and ideas previously separated by geography were brought closer through our command of this incredible technology.

The catalysts of greatest socioeconomic change have all had profound impact in improving human connectivity: the printing press, the telephone, the internet, etc. The U.S. railroad system created an unprecedented transportation network that ushered in a new era of prosperity unmatched in all of world history. Railroads literally laid the track toward making something as amazing as retirement possible!

There's an unmistakable, almost romantic allure to the visage of a steam locomotive. Everything about these mighty engines—their design, weight, power and speed—showcases the remarkableness of human ingenuity that's woven into our cultural fabric. It's pure Americana.

Wouldn't it be wonderful if planning for retirement were as easy as boarding a train? Your plan on a schedule, the destination set and the ride on smooth, steady rails. Can you picture it? When do you get on board? Where is your train taking you?

Planning for retirement isn't entirely unlike planning for a vacation. But too few people have an itinerary. It's understandable; retirement is complicated and requires the careful coordination of many issues. Pension and Social Security benefits need to be examined and maximized. Investment risks need to be measured and controlled. Medical insurance transition, coverage and budgeting requires careful execution. Taxes will need corralling and considerations should be made toward the efficient transfer of assets to your estate and beneficiaries.

Steam engines are complicated too. But their ability to transfer energy into forward momentum is directly attributable to the sum of their parts. Every gear and bolt has a place and role, deliberately placed by the engineer.

Retirement can achieve the same speed and grace but only under the coordination of a well-executed plan. This book will give you the background, understanding and tools needed to design the retirement of your dreams. Let's endeavor to lay the track toward your financial future on rails of steel.

Welcome aboard.

The first two chapters, **The Evolution of Retirement** and **The Grand Experiment,** explore the history of retirement to help the reader observe how retirement came to be, how far we've come and what challenges remain.

The next two chapters, **The Past Is Not Prologue** and **The Financial Toolbox,** examine the dangers of following antiquated retirement advice and stress the importance of approaching the planning process with an open mind. Current available tools, as well as their individual strengths and weaknesses, are covered.

The book is rounded out by taking an in-depth look at five key retirement planning components: **Income, Health Care, Inflation, Taxes** and **Estate Planning**. A retirement plan is only as strong as its weakest link, so considering all planning elements large and small is essential.

Your Ticket to Retirement explains our holistic planning process and details the benefits of teaming up with a qualified financial coach and fiduciary.

CHAPTER ONE

The Evolution of Retirement

"What walks on four legs in the morning, two at noon and three in the evening?"

—*the Riddle of the Sphinx*

Imagine your life depends on answering that riddle correctly. Take a moment; a lot is at stake!

In Greek myth, the Sphinx was a terrible monster with the body of a lion, the wings of an eagle and the head of a woman. Guarding the gates of Thebes, it taunted travelers with its riddle and devoured all who failed to solve it. Oedipus was the first to outsmart the beast by correctly answering its question: *the answer is Man.*

The riddle of the Sphinx poetically describes the entirety of our lives passing in a single day—we crawl on all fours as a baby, walk upright as an adult, but need the assistance of a walking stick in old age.

The road to retirement is little different—we spend our youth getting educated, save diligently for retirement as adults and with luck and preparation enjoy our golden years in peace and leisure. Along the way, we confront a variety of challenges and obstacles that shape our characters and life experiences. The benefits of all the good decisions made, or the consequences of all the mistakes, are often not realized for decades. A quality plan can make all the difference.

But if retirement is a natural part of life's path why are so many people worried about it? How is it that, after so much time, energy and collective expertise poured into one endeavor, we still struggle to find confidence in our financial future?

We live in a fast-paced world that's full of distractions; it's easy to procrastinate and delay the planning process to a time that continuously evades us. Others save too little, use poor investments or trust the wrong people. Some don't take the process seriously or assume that the government will solve all our problems.

But so much of the discourse on retirement ignores the fact that it's *evolving*. Just like our lives, retirement changes over time. Observing how retirement has taken shape over the years can give us clues to how it will continue to change in the future. After all, you don't know where you're going until you know where you've been.

Dying Too Soon ...

A hundred years ago, retirement didn't really exist, at least not as we know it today. If you weren't rich, you often worked until you dropped. Otherwise, your needs were met by children, extended family or the charity of others. There was no Social Security and few safety nets of any kind. Regardless, you wouldn't have been too worried about your "golden years." Prior to the 20th century, the average adult rarely lived beyond age 50.[1]

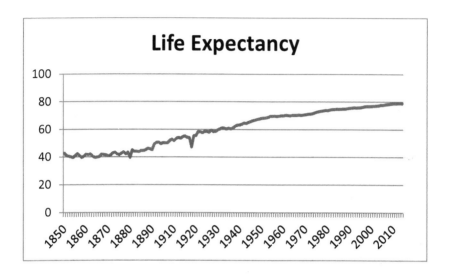

Getting old was a real challenge in a world where sanitation was rudimentary, good nutrition was a luxury and health care depended on how quickly you could reach a doctor by horse. Your greatest financial fear wasn't growing too old but *dying too soon*. An early death often meant financial hardship for a surviving spouse and children. Recognizing commercial opportunity, the life insurance industry blossomed during the late 19th century by appealing to the moral duty of husbands to provide financial security to their families.

---

[1] Centers for Disease Control. 2015. "Health, United States, 2015-Individual Charts and Tables: Spreadsheet, PDF, and PowerPoint files." https://www.cdc.gov/nchs/hus/contents2015.htm

By 1931, 55 percent of Americans were insured by over $109 billion of life insurance.[2] Americans vested an abiding faith in the protection that life insurance provided, especially after our involvement in the First World War. The loss of a family's primary breadwinner used to be an irrevocable and devastating economic loss, but, with each death claim paid, the insurance industry increasingly convinced Americans of the prudence of protection and planning.

During the Great Depression, because federal regulation prohibited life insurance companies from investing in stocks, the life insurance industry emerged from the economic collapse relatively unscathed. That stability helped to cement our trust in insurance as a cornerstone of financial planning. As you'll soon learn, this trust is central to the retirement story.

... Living Too Long

We truly live in blessed times. From the end of the 19th century to today, our quality of life has improved tremendously. Technological innovations in food production, manufacturing, transportation and health care have made the basics of everyday living more plentiful, affordable and readily available.

This innovation drastically improved life expectancy. Antibiotics, vaccinations and a decline in infant mortality rates were major contributors. As Americans began to reach advanced age in greater numbers, concern began to shift from dying too soon to *living too long*.

The Great Depression is often cited as the era during which retirement entered the national conversation. When the country fell on hard times, millions suffered—but older Americans were hit hardest. Jobs were scarce and this rapidly growing demographic had few options.

---

[2] CQ Researcher. May 19, 1933. "Life Insurance in the Depression." http://library.cqpress.com/cqresearcher/document.php?id=cqresrre1933051900

Many solutions were advanced. One that prompted widespread discussion was the proposal to provide a state pension for those aged 60 and older. While many in the federal government wanted to capitalize on this movement, there was staunch resistance to the creation of a program that some viewed as government-sponsored charity. A path toward compromise appeared when it was suggested the proposal be tweaked to have workers share in the cost of providing the societal safety net.

Still, the proposed legislation had fierce detractors. Some of the loudest dissent came from Americans who simply didn't want to pay additional taxes regardless of the supposed benefits. Proponents of the idea, cleverly taking advantage of the fact that Americans *already understood and trusted insurance*, positioned the payroll offset not as a tax but as a *premium* paid toward retirement income protection. Passed under the aptly named Federal *Insurance* Contributions Act (FICA), Social Security was born in 1935.

> **Fun Fact:** The first American to receive monthly Social Security benefits was Ida May Fuller of Vermont. She retired at 65, having paid just $25 into the system. Ida lived to 100 and collected $20,944, foreshadowing the difficulties that Social Security would encounter in the decades to come.

Taxes aside, the arrival of Social Security was received in rather lukewarm fashion. The reason may surprise you. Americans resisted retirement because it was considered boring! Having a job gave life purpose and allowed a person to keep busy while contributing to their family and community. Many shunned the thought of wasting away idly in a rocking chair. An 81-year old handyman once quipped to a reporter from the Chicago Tribune, "I don't have time to get bored or to feel old!"[3]

---

[3] Nancy McGill. Chicago Tribune. "Feb. 12, 1956. "Active Elders Snub Rocking Chair Futures: Keep Busy with Work, Hobbies or Service." http://archives.chicagotribune.com/1956/02/12/page/106/article/active-elders-snub-rocking-chair-futures.

Retirement Gets Redefined

As America emerged from the Depression and the benefits of Social Security began circulating among the older population, the rich and famous led the way in redefining retirement. They abandoned their rocking chairs and tied advanced age to leisure-time activities! Country clubs and golf courses spread like wildfire.

People in the 1930s were no less enamored with celebrity culture than we are today. Media of every type—radio, magazines, newspapers, movies and especially the exciting new medium of television celebrated retirement as a break from tedium and toil. Folks from every band of the economic spectrum found new ways to keep occupied. Over time retirement culture adopted additional mainstays such as Florida living, migratory arrangements, motor homes, retirement communities and more.

Retirement, embracing the pursuit of idleness, took on entirely new meaning. It became as American as apple pie and promised everyone who worked hard and planned carefully the gifts it had to offer.

CHAPTER TWO

The Grand Experiment: Pensions, Social Security and the 401(k)

"If at first you don't succeed, try, try again!"
−W.E. Hickson

top and consider: retirement as we define it today has only been around for two, going on three generations. We've struggled to develop a model to answer retirement's fundamental question:

how do we sustainably support a person's retirement in the face of increasing life expectancy?

Making Retirement Work

History shows that wholesale changes to the way we live is often contentious and typically resisted. Just consider our track record on civil rights, Prohibition, taxation, health care and welfare. It's been a roller coaster and there's little consensus; most of these topics are still subject to heated debate today!

It's no different with retirement. Each proposal to solve the puzzle of supporting longevity has been met with skepticism, debate and challenges. Many attempts at creating sustainable retirement income have crumbled or become obsolete. Even now, some people trust their fortunes to financial vehicles that are likely to fail or be detrimental to their goals. This is not unlike Wile E. Coyote chasing the Road Runner. With each attempt he gets cleverer, daring and seemingly closer to his goal. But his prize is always just out of reach and the poor coyote ends up mangled and bruised.

We're in the middle of what I like to call the Grand Retirement Experiment—the quest to find the best strategy to move all of society through a comfortable, sustainable retirement. So far, we've tested pensions, Social Security and the 401(k). How have things worked out?

The Corporate Solution

Let's start at the beginning—pensions.

Historically, the inability to work was a major problem. Without family or charitable support, people would find themselves destitute. But the problem doesn't stop there; poverty is a societal problem. If too many people are without the means to support themselves, it can foment crime, public health issues and social unrest.

Rome in 13 BC was an empire that had conquered much of the known world. Emperor Augustus understood that he had created a large body of veterans from all the empire building. When these soldiers could no longer fight, they stopped getting paid.

Idle soldiers without a steady source of income were a major risk. They could create political instability or instigate a coup. Out of necessity Emperor Augustus created the *aerarium militare*—a treasury with the sole purpose of providing pensions for veterans who served 20 years or more in the regular army.

Seventeen centuries later, the military pension found its way to American soil when the Continental Congress enacted a law that covered all officers, soldiers and sailors, providing them income if they became disabled while serving. Later, at the behest of General Washington, the military pension was expanded to provide lifetime income to his officers following retiring from the army. This was intended to compensate them for sacrificing better-income earning opportunities in the private sector, and in gratitude for their service.

Our young country was primarily a nation of farmers. Men worked as long as they could and then turned the land over to the next generation. In 1880, half of all Americans were employed on farms and 78 percent of men who lived beyond age 65 worked.[4]

Later, as the industrial revolution took root, both men and women left the farm to work in factories. Labor was plentiful, but as the saying goes, good help was hard to find. Business owners began casting about for ways to discourage turnover and keep talented employees from straying.

---

[4] Joanna Short. Augustana College, Economic History Association. "Economic History of Retirement in the United States." https://eh.net/encyclopedia/economic-history-of-retirement-in-the-united-states/.

In 1875, the pension officially migrated from the military to the private sector when the American Express Company created a retirement plan that allowed employees to receive income after retirement based on their average salary, duration of employment and retirement age. Since income at retirement could be calculated based upon those qualifying factors, the plans were dubbed "defined-benefit" plans. The pension was primed to go mainstream.

During the next 100 years private companies established more than 500 private pensions. By 1975 these pensions covered nearly half of all American workers.[5] The plans were immensely popular as they allowed employees to retire with a predictable and guaranteed source of lifetime income. The pension served as the *premier* retirement platform for nearly the entire 20th century.

Then, just as baby boomers were beginning their careers, pension plans started becoming frozen, reduced or canceled. If pensions were so universally loved, why were they being taken away?

Bye-bye Pensions

The answer is complicated. But we can identify some major contributors:

Legislative — In 1974 Congress passed the Employee Retirement Income Security Act (ERISA). Prior to its passage, pension providers mostly policed themselves, in some instances badly or not at all. ERISA established specific requirements addressing participation, vesting, funding and reporting to ensure that pensions were being managed prudently. These requirements, while ultimately good, were also conservative in nature, increasing the costs associated with maintaining a pension plan.

Shareholder Pressure — The interests of a company's shareholders and its employees can be very different. Shareholders seek

---

[5] Patrick W. Seburn. Bureau of Labor Statistics, Monthly Labor Review. December 1991. "Evolution of employer-provided defined benefit pensions." https://www.bls.gov/opub/mlr/1991/12/art3full.pdf.

the highest possible return on their investment, which encourages a business to maximize revenues while reducing costs. Employees generally want to receive compensation and benefits reflective of the perceived value of their labor. When pension costs began to rise because of ERISA legislation, shareholders of many firms petitioned to reduce or eliminate benefits.

Longevity — The increase in life expectancy may be the greatest contributor to the demise of pensions. In 1900, the average worker made it to age 50. By the year 2000, this figure skyrocketed to 80, drastically increasing pension funding requirements and the benefits paid. In just a few decades, pensions morphed from a great employee retention tool into a crushing business expense.

Unrealistic Expectations — Pension plan managers became desperate to find creative ways to offset rising costs. One solution was to make pension reserve funds work harder. This was accomplished by seeking greater investment returns, which of course required taking greater risks. Pension funds flocked into the stock and bond markets where it was assumed that higher rates of return could be achieved. At first, the markets delivered. But over the past 20 years interest rates plummeted while market volatility increased. The lack of predictable rates of return has only exacerbated pension problems.

In combination, these factors have produced some devastating results. Moody's Investor Service estimates that total unfunded liabilities of U.S. state pensions will reach $1.75 trillion in 2017.[6] Other sources indicate the problem could be significantly worse,

---

[6] Reuters. Oct. 7, 2016. "U.S. state public pension unfunded liabilities to hit $1.75 trillion: Moody's." http://www.cnbc.com/2016/10/07/us-state-public-pension-unfunded-liabilities-to-hit-175-trillion-moodys.html.

with some estimating that liabilities might be as high as $5 trillion![7] Private pensions aren't faring much better. The underfunded liabilities of just the companies in the S&P 1500 are estimated to be $562 billion.[8]

To borrow a phrase from the 60s, "this is such a bummer," because people love pensions. Ask a pensioner if they would trade theirs in for a 401(k) and chances are they'll tell you, "No way!" When you're retired there's no greater peace of mind than a steady and dependable source of income.

But, like it or not, pensions are going away. And many people counting on those defined-benefit plans will see their checks reduced or, in some cases, disappear entirely as the consequences of poor management come home to roost.

Social Security — The Government Solution

Germany was the first nation to offer government-sponsored retirement insurance. In 1889, Chancellor Otto von Bismarck convinced the Reichstag that "those who are disabled from work by age and invalidity have a well-grounded claim to care from the state." It would be another 54 years before President Franklin Delano Roosevelt would import the same concept to the United States.

When it comes to understanding Social Security, it's helpful to begin by considering the one constant about the program that's been true since its inception: it was *never* designed to cover 100 percent of your retirement income

---

[7] Andrew Biggs. Forbes. July 1, 2016. "Opinion: Are State and Local Government Pensions Underfunded by $5 Trillion?" https://www.forbes.com/sites/andrewbiggs/2016/07/01/are-state-and-local-government-pensions-underfunded-by-5-trillion/#3c7d875d157f.

[8] George Will. Feb. 22, 2017. "America's Utterly Predictable Tsunami of Pension Problems." https://www.washingtonpost.com/opinions/americas-utterly-predictable-tsunami-of-pension-problems/2017/02/22/1e5de00e-f869-11e6-9845-576c69081518_story.html?utm_term=.1e095a1a8f9d.

needs. In fact, many Americans were never expected to collect Social Security at all.

In 1935, when the program was introduced, the age at which you could begin collecting was set at 65. At that time, the average American lived to 61. That's right—Washington was banking on many Americans not living long enough to collect benefits! Even FDR, the sitting president who introduced the program, died when he was 63.

This isn't to suggest that Social Security was created to hoodwink the people. Remember the context: the Great Depression had the nation questioning how seniors would be cared for as longevity continued to improve. But Americans were no fonder of taxes then than we are today and were wary of handing over the reins to the retirement safety net to the state.

Social "Security"?

As noted earlier, to soften the impression of increased taxes, Social Security payments were characterized as "premiums" for "insurance" to be collected at an advanced age. Understanding that Social Security was pitched as insurance is important. Not everything in life is insurable; very specific criteria needs to be met.

Most insurable risks must be catastrophic in nature, such that people will want protection from it. Examples include a home fire, wrecking an automobile and possibly injuring others, passing away and leaving dependents financially destitute, etc. Catastrophic protection is the reason most Americans have homeowners, auto and life insurance. Running out of money in retirement is every bit as catastrophic.

But it's also important for insurable risk to be *rare.* Most homes don't burn down, most drivers reach their destinations safely every day and most people do not die prematurely. Rarity is crucial. It allows premiums thrown into the common pot to be small and affordable, since the expectation is only an unlucky few will need to collect.

But if a risk is common enough to be *anticipated*, nearly everyone will end up dipping into the pot. Insuring against a common, anticipated risk demands skyrocketing premiums as the cost of protection begins to approach the actual cost of incurring the risk! This is a major frustration and should sound somewhat familiar. The contentious debate we are having in our country right now about the difficulty of making health insurance affordable stems from this very issue.

When Social Security launched, the odds of an American collecting benefits for a long period of time was rare. In 1935, the average American lived to 61. The segment of the population that made it beyond 65 only lived another 13 years, on average. **Today, 90 percent of Americans are expected to make it to age 65. And those who do can expect to live another 20 years, on average![9] So here's our problem: retirement is no longer rare but *commonplace*.**

Increased life expectancy causes another problem. The ratio between those collecting benefits and those contributing to the common pot has become badly skewed. In 1935, there were more than 150 workers supporting every Social Security recipient. That sounds strong and dependable. By 1950, just 15 years later, that ratio sank to 16 to 1! Today there are fewer than *three* workers supporting every retiree. [10] We simply are not collecting enough FICA tax to meet the demand for benefits. This issue will only get worse as technology and medicine continue to improve.

---

[9] Andy Kiersz. Business Insider. March 21, 2014. "This is When You're Going to Die." http://www.businessinsider.com/social-security-life-table-charts-2014-3.

[10] Social Security. 2013. "Social Security History: Frequently Asked Questions: Ratio of Covered Workers to Beneficiaries." https://www.ssa.gov/history/ratios.html.

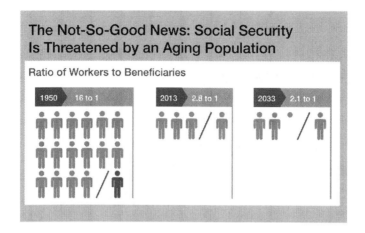

Social Security must be overhauled. The cracks and weaknesses are plain to see. But I believe that politicians are ignoring serious discussion of the problem. We just endured a multi-year presidential campaign, yet, among all the debates and platforming, absolutely no meaningful proposals to fix Social Security emerged. Certainly, major candidates promised to preserve benefits and in some instances to expand them, but that's not problem-solving, it's pandering in my view.

But Washington is not ignorant of the problem. Benefits have been quietly getting reduced to alleviate budgetary imbalances. In three of the last eight years Congress has failed to offer a cost of living adjustment (COLA) for retirees.[11] Worse, the Bipartisan Budget Act of 2015 stripped away marital switching strategies.

For years, a married person could defer their own Social Security benefit, letting it earn 8 percent in annual credits until age 70, but collect up to 50 percent of their spouse's benefit in the interim. Proper use of this strategy could increase lifetime Social Security income for married couples by 10-30 percent! But unless you

---

[11] Social Security Administration. 2017. "Cost-Of-Living Adjustments." https://www.ssa.gov/oact/cola/colaseries.html.

turned age 62 by the end of 2015, this strategy was taken away by recent legislation.

> **The Fine Print:** Evidence for Social Security's woes has been right under your nose for years. Have you ever noticed the disclaimer that appears on the second page of every Social Security statement? It currently reads:
>
> "Your estimated benefits are based on current law. Congress has made changes to the law in the past and can do so at any time. The law governing benefit amounts may change because, by 2034, the payroll taxes collected will be enough to pay only about 79 percent of scheduled benefits."

Then there is this excerpt from the 2014 Trustees Report:

> Social Security is not sustainable over the long term at current benefit and tax rates. In 2010, the program paid more in benefits and expenses than it collected in taxes and other noninterest income, and the 2014 Trustees Report projects this pattern to continue for the next 75 years. [12]

We deserve a more open and honest discussion about the fate of Social Security. But in 2017, I believe that politicians are demonstrating a complete inability or unwillingness to address the problem. With corporate pensions disappearing and Social Security appearing to "circle the drain", so to speak, you might be wondering who is going to be responsible for making retirement work. Look in the mirror!

The 401(k) — You're on Your Own

The birth of the 401(k) took place in a tiny suburb near Philadelphia in 1980. Ted Benna worked for the Johnson Companies, a

---

[12] Social Security Board of Trustees. July 28, 2014. "2014 Annual Report of the Board of Trustees of the Federal Old-Age and Survivors Insurance and Federal Disability Insurance Trust Funds." https://www.ssa.gov/oact/TR/2014/tr2014.pdf.

firm that created, implemented and managed executive benefit plans.

Ted was a devout Christian and found his work at odds with his faith. He was troubled that his corporate clients were richly rewarding executives while doing nothing for rank-and-file employees. What Ted decided to do about it would change the nature of retirement forever.

While contemplating leaving the business to find another vocation better aligned with his principles, he noticed an obscure provision in the Internal Revenue Code. While subsection 401(k) was designed to limit perks to corporate executives, it could also allow employees to save for their future on a pre-tax basis. There was even room to incentivize companies to match their employees' contributions by making those dollars tax deductible.

Ted and his co-workers asked the IRS to approve his interpretation and succeeded in 1981. Within a year, the Johnson Companies were administering 401(k) plans for 50 other businesses. Growth was explosive; by 1983, nearly half of all large employers were either offering a 401(k) or considering doing so according to the Employee Benefit Research Institute.[13] By 1996, 401(k) plans could boast over 30 million participants and more than $1 trillion dollars invested![14]

The timing of the 401(k) was perfect for corporate America. Already desperate to distance themselves from the ballooning burden of pension obligations, along came a solution that put responsibility for retirement funding squarely on the shoulders of employees.

---

[13] Tom Anderson. LearnVest. July 3, 2013. "Your 401(k): When It Was Invented—and Why." https://www.learnvest.com/knowledge-center/your-401k-when-it-was-invented-and-why/.

[14] Ibid.

Today, more than 94 percent of employers offer 401(k), 403(b), TSA, SEP, SIMPLE IRA or similar qualified plans.[15] But what's the big difference between these and pensions? There are *no* defined benefits.

The plans described above are called defined-*contribution* plans. All that's known are the amounts contributed by individual employees. Sure, many employers pitch in by providing a match, but the end result is uncertain.

Pensions are popular because they are defined-*benefit* plans. Employees know *exactly* what they'll receive in retirement benefits well in advance. The benefit of a 401(k) fluctuates, sometimes wildly, depending on individual investment strategies. **There's a big difference between working toward a defined goal versus one that is entirely unpredictable.**

There's no doubt that the 401(k) is currently expected to be the vehicle that carries baby boomers and subsequent generations through retirement. Knowing this, we should survey the current state of the Grand Retirement Experiment. How has it worked out for America now that we've effectively replaced the pension with the 401(k)?

The result may not be the panacea we imagined. Even Ted Benna expressed regret in 2011, "(the) monster is out of control. I would blow up the system and restart with something totally different." Why are Ted and others so concerned? The 401(k) has a lot of flaws:

Complexity: Originally, 401(k) plans "could be explained to employees in just a minute," said Benna. "There were two options, a guaranteed fund and an equity fund."[16] But, as the plans went mainstream, sophisticated investors demanded more options, which complicated things for the average, less savvy participant.

---

[15] Ibid.

[16] Jeremy Olshan. Smart Money. Nov. 22, 2011. "'Father' of the 401(k)'s Tough Love." http://blogs.smartmoney.com/encore/2011/11/22/father-of-the-401ks-tough-love.

"We went to three options, then to six, then to seven, then to 15—it is far beyond what most participants were able to deal with," Benna said. "And I am not convinced we have added value by getting more complicated."

This complexity has two potentially problematic consequences. First, it tempts participants into making bad decisions such as picking inappropriate investments or panic selling. The second and more problematic consequence is that complexity intimidates many employees to the extent they do not participate at all.

Underfunding: According to the Employee Benefit Research Institute the average American retirement nest egg has a median value of $60,000.[17] To zero in on baby boomers, a Government Accountability Office (GAO) study conducted in 2015 found the average retirement nest egg accumulated by 55-to-64-year-olds was just $104,000.[18]

If that amount were transformed into a lifetime annuity, it would generate approximately $310 per month. This is far short of what is needed to complement Social Security to provide lifetime income. Left to their own devices, Americans are not saving enough.

Poor Performance: High fees and bad decision-making has created a pretty poor track record for 401(k) performance. A 2016 Dalbar study found the average investor earned a 4.7 percent average annual return over the past 15 years when, over the same period, the S&P 500 returned 8.2 percent.[19]

---

[17] Kathleen Elkins. CNBC. Sept. 12, 2016. "Here's How Much the Average American Family Has Saved for Retirement." http://www.cnbc.com/2016/09/12/heres-how-much-the-average-american-family-has-saved-for-retirement.html.

[18] U.S. Government Accountability Office. May 12, 2015. "Most Households Approaching Retirement Have Low Savings." http://www.gao.gov/products/GAO-15-419.

[19] Dalbar. 2016. "Dalbar's 22nd Annual Quantitative Analysis of Investor Behavior." http://www.qidllc.com/wp-content/uploads/2016/02/2016-Dalbar-QAIB-Report.pdf.

Investors tend to get in and out of the market at the wrong times. Pension plans put professional money managers in charge of investment decisions, while 401(k) plans place these same decisions in the hands of people with limited experience.

High Fees: "The 401(k) is one of the only products that Americans buy that they don't know the price of," says Teresa Ghilarducci, an economist and nationally recognized expert on retirement security. According to a study by the National Association of Retirement Plan Participants, 58 percent of participants don't even know they're paying fees on their workplace retirement accounts. [20]

There are mutual fund fees, administrative costs, transaction costs, redemption fees, soft-dollar costs, advisor commissions and more. It might be reasonable to pay about 1 percent, but investors frequently pay 3-4 percent after factoring in disclosed fees, hidden fees, trading costs and tax inefficiencies. [21] That difference may seem small, but the impact can be staggering.

Because of the power of compounding interest, an extra 2 percent paid in fees will translate to a *50 percent* smaller account size over a 30-year period! Wall Street continues to benefit at the expense of our ignorance. Should we have expected anything else? [22]

---

[20] National Association of Retirement Plan Participants. June 2, 2015. "42 Million People Do Not Know They Are Paying Any Fees on Their Workplace Retirement Plans." http://www.ireachcontent.com/news-releases/42-million-people-do-not-know-they-are-paying-any-fees-on-their-workplace-retirement-plans-505809961.html.

[21] Kenneth Kim. Forbes. Sept. 24, 2016. "How Much Do Mutual Funds Really Cost." https://www.forbes.com/sites/kennethkim/2016/09/24/how-much-do-mutual-funds-really-cost/#7d95f35ba527.

[22] The S&P 500 is an unmanaged index of 500 American stock companies and it is not possible to invest in the index directly. The performance of the S&P 500 does not reflect the deduction of investment fees or charges, which would reduce the return shown here.

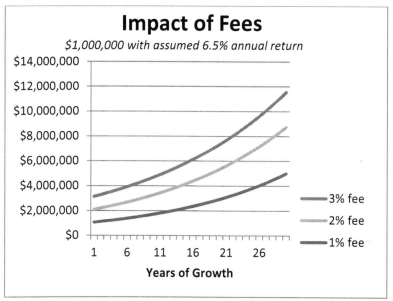

This example is hypothetical only and does not reflect the deduction of specific products fees and expenses or income taxes, which would reduce the figures shown here.

Waning Momentum: The introduction of the 401(k) ushered in the opportunity for middle Americans to more meaningfully and consistently participate in the stock market. This naturally increased the demand for stocks, which pushed stock prices higher in the ensuing decades as the 401(k) gained in popularity.

The 80s and 90s mark the greatest bull market in history, with annualized returns sometimes exceeding 19 percent. Part of that amazing growth can be directly attributed to the massive influx of new investors and capital. But that great burst in momentum has leveled off and the market has noticeably flagged, coupled with increased volatility in recent years.

Grand Retirement Experiment: The Results

For all the reasons covered, it appears the Grand Retirement Experiment hasn't worked out so well for many Americans. People love their pensions; they represent a promise to provide lifetime retirement income. And who funds the pension? The employer, mostly. Who takes the risk? The employer. Who is responsible for making the money last a lifetime? The employer. But the pension is going the way of the dodo.

We've replaced pensions with 401(k) and similar plans, which I like to call YO-YOs. That's an acronym that stands for *You're On Your Own.* Why?

Who funds the 401(k) plan? You do. Who takes the risk? You do. Who is responsible for making the money last a lifetime? You are. Employers, seeing their costs soar due to increased longevity, pulled pensions in favor of 401(k) plans. This game has changed entirely and the burden of providing lifetime income sits squarely on your shoulders.

CHAPTER THREE

The Past Is Not Prologue

"Whatever made you successful in the past won't in the future."
–Lewis E. Platt

To conclude our history lesson, I want to share a word on history itself. Most retirement advice is based on historic experience or performance. How many investments do you own right now because you expect the future performance to be similar to what's happened in the recent past? My guess is nearly *everything* you've got is positioned on this premise. I've got news for you: the next 30 years are going to be *entirely unlike* the past 30 years.

While historical data is useful for some things, being the only real guide we have, it's also severely flawed in other aspects. To be of any real value, data should be abundant. Would you take a drug if it had only been tested on a couple of people? Pharmaceuticals don't even pass a Phase 3 clinical trial without being tested on thousands of patients.[23] Stock market data is only available going back to 1870; that may seem like a long time, but it only gives us about 150 years of data to observe.

It also helps if data is comparable. For instance, we can only judge the efficacy of a drug if it's tested on people who all have the same illness. If everyone tested has a different ailment, how could you possibly judge with accuracy what kind of effect the drug is having? Similarly, is it remotely fair to compare the economy of 1870 to 2017? Absolutely not! During that stretch, any two decades in comparison may or may not share the U.S. highway system, commercial air travel or the internet in common. Looking backward much further than 30 years is like observing an alien world!

And, let's face it, the United States experienced incredible economic growth throughout the 20th century. I see no reason to expect this expansion to repeat. Seventy years ago, most of Western civilization was in rubble in the wake of World War II. The United States, safely buffered by two enormous oceans, emerged unscathed and raced off unchecked to become the dominant global economic powerhouse. The effects of this prosperity have reached far and wide. Enormous wealth circulated, giving life to a burgeoning middle class. Life expectancy skyrocketed and saving enough money to provide for a retirement of leisure became a real possibility for the first time in history.

But things have *changed*. I love this county and still believe we clearly lead the way in innovation, but we've got two enormous

---

[23] U.S. Food & Drug Administration. Nov. 6, 2014. "Inside Clinical Trials: Testing Medical Products in People." https://www.fda.gov/Drugs/ResourcesForYou/Consumers/ucm143531.htm.

headwinds that simply cannot be ignored. According to the U.S. Census Bureau, the fastest-growing population segment in our country is people over the age of 85.[24] We can't look to history for guidance on how to contend with a rapidly aging population; this is unprecedented! If anything, this reality will further strain the other big concern: our country's debt obligations.

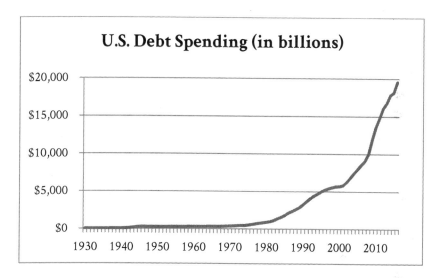

U.S. Debt Spending (in billions)

It took our country over 200 years to accrue its first trillion dollars of debt in 1981. Within just 25 more years of that benchmark, largely in response to the banking crisis, the tally would breach 10 trillion. What's fascinating is that in the subsequent decade, despite being told that the economy is recovering splendidly, the national debt is on course to *double* and breach 20 trillion in 2017.[25]

---

[24] United States Census Bureau. Nov. 30, 2011. "2010 Census Shows 65 and Older Population Growing Faster Than Total U.S. Population." https://www.census.gov/newsroom/releases/archives/2010_census/cb11-cn192.html.

[25] FRED Economic Data. May 2017. "Federal Debt: Total Public Debt." https://fred.stlouisfed.org/series/GFDEBTN.

An aging population combined with rising debt is going to cause trouble. At the very least, we should expect higher taxes to service the interest on the debt and the demands that our aging population will place on Social Security and Medicare. Higher taxes constrain economic activity, which of course affects investment based on that activity.

The evidence is already all around us. Consider that the generation referred to as the "Greatest Generation" retired *en masse* in the late 1970s and early 1980s. At that time, retirees seeking a safe rate of return could turn to their local bank branch. The average five-year CD rate in 1984 was 11 percent.[26] Those with a greater appetite for risk, investing in the U.S. stock market, might have experienced significant rates of return as the S&P 500 skyrocketed by 1,260 percent between 1980 and 1999. That's without counting dividends!

What a great time to retire! Money seemed to do nothing but grow. Pensions were abundant. Health care began to reach its pinnacle in terms of quality, accessibility and affordability. The Greatest Generation seemed to have retired into near perfect conditions.

But notice the marked differences in these same conditions as baby boomers approach retirement. The new millennium began with an epic crash — the bursting of the dot-com bubble. Massive growth in housing fueled a recovery, but also set up the next debacle—the financial collapse of 2008. The stock market was effectively stagnant over this stretch, earning the moniker "the lost decade."[27]

The tepid recovery we find ourselves in today has come at a cost. Our country has borrowed relentlessly from the future to stimulate the present. Interest rates have been suppressed to record lows for

---

[26] Denise Mazzucco. Bankrate. April 19, 2016. "Historical CD Interest Rates—1984-2016." http://www.bankrate.com/banking/cds/historical-cd-interest-rates-1984-2016.

[27] David Weidner. The Wall Street Journal. Oct. 15, 2009. "The Lost Decade of Stock Investing." https://www.wsj.com/articles/SB125556534569686215.

more than eight years. Interest rates near zero are great for borrowers, but horrible for savers. The average five-year CD rate was 0.86 percent in 2016. [28]

This dismal stretch of returns in both risk- and protection-oriented assets has contributed to the large reduction of pensions which, for many, have been slashed, frozen or withdrawn. According to the U.S. Bureau of Labor Statistics, participants in defined-benefit pension plans fell from 28 percent of the workforce in 1979 to 2 percent by 2013. [29] Making matters worse, by the government's own admission, we know that, absent a major overhaul, the Social Security Trust Fund will near depletion while baby boomers are in the middle of retirement, requiring major changes, tax increases or reduced benefits for the program's survival.

These realities cast a grim picture. But it's not unprecedented. Countries and cultures move through periods of boom and bust. Such is the rhythm of history. But the point of this review is simple. You need to think differently to navigate retirement successfully. The retirement playbook your parents' generation followed likely won't apply in your situation.

This is not to say you can't invest in the future and do so fearlessly. But we need to discard analysis, opinion or prognostication predicated solely on the past. Unfortunately, this is a hallmark of the financial industry. Marketing departments love to have you focus on the rearview mirror because the past was so *good*. But buried in the fine print of almost every financial brochure or advertisement is that familiar disclosure: *Past performance is not an indicator of future results.*

I don't have all the answers. Predicting the future is a fool's errand. But we are entering entirely uncharted waters. We've never

---

[28] Denise Mazzucco. Bankrate. April 19, 2016. "Historical CD Interest Rates—1984-2016." http://www.bankrate.com/banking/cds/historical-cd-interest-rates-1984-2016.

[29] Employee Benefit Research Institute. "FAQs About Benefits—Retirement Issues." https://www.ebri.org/publications/benfaq/index.cfm?fa=retfaq14.

retired so many people so quickly into an environment likely to be marked by heightened volatility and uncertainty.

Some Serious Questions:

- What happens if government and employer-sponsored benefits are reduced or eliminated?
- How do we prepare for future health care needs given increasing costs?
- Should we expect higher taxes due to record deficits?
- If You're On Your Own, how can you confidently make your nest egg last 20, 30 or even 40 years?
- Where do you put money when interest rates are in the gutter and the stock market behaves like a buzz saw?

Retirement planning starts with determination. The challenges are immense but they are not insurmountable. It's time to get proactive and educated. There's no sense in waiting for politicians, bureaucrats or financial wizards to show us the path to salvation. Many of them orchestrated the current mess!

Getting Your Ticket to Retirement

Subsequent chapters will give you a blueprint to follow so you can get your retirement on track and on time. The plan is simple and fully explains many of the tools and strategies available. Along our journey, we'll stop and explore these five core retirement planning elements:

Income — When the paychecks stop you need a plan to provide a replacement stream of income capable of lasting a lifetime. Next, you'll want to protect that income from taking a **HIT**. That's an acronym representing the three primary risks seeking to separate you from your hard-earned money:

Healthcare — Plan for Medicare transition. Know what it covers and, more importantly, what it does not.

<u>I</u>nflation — The stealthiest of risks, inflation robs you of your standard of living over time. It's crucial that your income grows to keep inflation at bay.

<u>T</u>axes — When you're on a fixed income, few things are more discouraging than your tax obligations. To a certain extent, taxes are unavoidable, but they can be tamed.

Legacy — If you don't live long enough to spend all your money, who benefits? In the absence of a plan, it might very well be the government. But, with a little forethought, you can direct the money to the kids, family or charity of your choice, where it belongs.

Let's get started!

The Financial Toolbox

"Nothing is perfect. Outcomes are uncertain. People are irrational."
–Hugh Mackay

As we begin to lay the foundation for planning your financial future we will introduce overarching concepts and strategies. We'll also discuss specific investment vehicles designed to help reduce or eliminate certain retirement risks. We may challenge some of your preconceptions and biases. We'll even question some things you've heard about the role of certain financial products in your financial portfolio.

Retirement planning can generate passionate debate. Financial advisors, money managers and economists have argued for decades about the best ways to deploy money. Another contributor to this dispute is the abysmal record financial professionals have in predicting the future.

There's no stopping industry "experts" from engaging in endless speculation about which financial products will perform best in the future. That's why we strongly suggest you ignore this chatter because it's just NOISE.

Of equal importance, avoid the directives of absolutists, my term for "experts" who only promote one thing. You'll often find them insisting that their strategy is the *only* way to go while other specific strategies should *never* be used in any circumstance. There's an abundance of these characters singing the singular praises of stock market investing, annuities, insurance strategies and the like. Absolutists are fools or have an agenda, in my view. Here's why:

Just Tools

Financial vehicles are just tools. Every tool has a specific purpose that can be made useful in some contexts and useless in others. Would you ever rummage through a contractor's toolbox, pluck out a wrench and declare it useless? Would you say, "Wrenches are terrible! Suze Orman says that hammers are much better!"? Of course not.

Wrenches and hammers have totally different purposes. If I'm fixing a leaky faucet, I'm probably going to need that wrench. But if I'm driving nails, I'm going to need the hammer. And they *both* belong in a well-equipped toolbox.

So why would we apply absolutist thinking to investments? Why would we trust an advisor or guru who praises one financial vehicle while deprecating another? Unfortunately, many of us do this all the time for somewhat understandable reasons.

The first is cultural. We live in a highly-polarized society and everybody picks a side. Red states versus blue states. Burgers or pizza. Patriots fans versus the entire NFL (sorry, couldn't resist). No matter how mundane (or serious) the subject, people like choosing a side and hurling rocks at everything on the other side of the fence.

The second—and more perilous—reason behind absolutist thinking is that, like it or not, certain people and companies in the financial services industry have an agenda. This agenda is not always aligned with the consumer's individual needs.

Lo and behold! Many singing the praises of mutual funds sell nothing else to earn commissions. Others warning you of the dangers of annuities may not even be licensed to sell them. I've consulted hundreds of times with clients who've worked for years with "unbiased" financial advisors, only to review their portfolios and find them full of proprietary products from the advisor's parent company.

Advisors, experts and gurus—being human—have agendas, egos, predictions they'd like to see made accurate, sales quotas to meet and families to feed. These influences can affect and even distort advice delivered by otherwise fine professionals.

Planning Tip: The best way to ensure that the advice you're receiving is in your best interest is to work with a fiduciary. A fiduciary has a legal responsibility to put your needs and interests ahead of their own. Many financial representatives are serving the solicitation interests of a parent company or firm.

Certified Financial Planner™ is a designation earned by individuals who have met rigorous professional standards and have agreed to adhere to the principles of integrity, objectivity, competence, fairness, confidentiality, professionalism and diligence when dealing with clients. CFP® advisors who engage in financial planning services are held to the fiduciary standard by the CFP® Board's standards of professional conduct. Likewise, all Registered Investment Advisor professionals are regulated as fiduciaries by the Securities and Exchange Commission (SEC) or appropriate state securities regulator.

Be sure to do your homework. There are bad apples even amongst carefully groomed subsets of professionals, and fiduciaries are no different. But shopping within this space is a great place to start.

Simply put, financial tools have specific purposes that work in specific situations. Consideration of any tool should be made independent of any quota, commission, sales contest, ego or agenda. Just like any other walk of life, it's important to identify the right tools for the job. In considering retirement, certain tools will become more appealing based on your age, goals and tolerance for risk.

Never choose an index fund, an annuity, T-notes or even a CD simply because someone tells you it's the only way to go and that everything else is wrong. Without a deep understanding of your needs and resources, this kind of advice is lazy at best and dangerous at worst.

Cracking the Lid

It's time to open the financial toolbox and learn more about the tools available. But first, a word on the common limitation shared by all financial solutions:

Without exception, <u>ALL</u> financial vehicles are flawed.

Every tool in our financial toolbox has pros and cons, strengths and weaknesses, benefits and limitations. There are *no* exceptions.

If there *were* a perfect financial vehicle, what would it look like? I'd propose it'd have these three attributes:

Growth — A perfect financial vehicle would grow consistently over time. We all want our money to multiply.

Protection — A perfect financial vehicle would eliminate risk of loss. People hate to lose money. Our perfect product would feature protection of principal and interest earned.

Control — A perfect financial vehicle would be accessible at whim with no "gotchas." We want to spend, move, count and distribute our money however and whenever we want with little in the way of fees, penalties and limitations.

Did I miss anything? Maybe. Perfection is in the eye of the dreamer. But I hope you agree that a product that features growth, protection and control in one neat package would make for a fantastic retirement foundation.

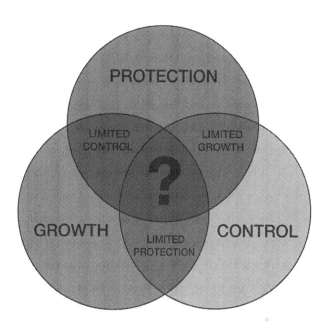

I hate to take the candy away, but this perfect product doesn't exist. This shouldn't come as a surprise. If a perfect financial product existed, you'd already know about it and have all your money stowed within. The good news is many financial solutions feature any two of the attributes described, *but almost always at the expense of the third.* As we explore the financial toolbox, this theme will become clearer. However, it's what you *do* with this information that makes all the difference.

The products we're concerned with in this book comprise the more commonly used vehicles for retirement planning. Three primary financial institutions offer these tools: Wall Street, banks and insurance companies. Let's explore.

Wall Street

Get ready; we're headed to the casino. But this is a unique gambling experience. If you play with your money long enough in Vegas, you're mathematically certain to walk away with empty pockets. But in many cases, the Wall Street "casino" has historically *rewarded* investors who hang around for the long-term while being broadly diversified.

But coming away a winner isn't so straightforward. Wall Street offers an opportunity to make a fortune ... or lose one. *When* you start investing, in *what* amounts, the *decisions* you make (or don't) along the stretch and, especially, how *withdrawals* are timed can drastically alter your outcome.

This isn't your grandfather's stock market. High -frequency trading, aggressive global and domestic monetary policy, dubious securitization, lackluster regulation, trading algorithms and complicated geopolitics serve to alter the investor experience and enhance volatility. It's vital to ask yourself as you approach retirement: "How much risk am I willing to take?"

Stocks — A share of stock represents fractional ownership in a publicly traded company. If you own any shares of Apple, Johnson & Johnson or Exxon Mobil, you participate in the rewards and risks of being an owner of the company. If the new iPhone sells like hotcakes, your ownership stake is likely to increase. However, if Exxon causes an environmental catastrophe, the value of your holdings may fall.

Stocks have a fascinating history. The first exchange opened in Antwerp, Belgium, in 1460. There are now more than 16 domestic and international exchanges with market capitalization of $1 trillion or more, the largest of which is the New York Stock Exchange.

> **Fun fact:** Ever wonder how Wall Street got its name? A 12-foot wooden stockade was laid across lower Manhattan in 1685 to protect Dutch settlers from British and Native American attacks. These days, I think some Americans might feel better-protected if the sharks and wolves of Wall Street were walled in!

Over time, there have been few investments with higher returns than the U.S. stock market. Conversely, in the short term, it's also been one of the best places to lose money. Stocks can be a very risky investment. Given this uncertainty, most people seek to mitigate that risk as retirement nears.

A debate that has raged for decades is whether holding stock qualifies as speculation or investment. Part of the problem is defining the difference. In his book *Where Are the Customer's Yachts?* Fred Schwed Jr. attempted the distinction this way, **"Speculation is an effort, probably unsuccessful, to turn a little money into a lot. Investing is an effort, which should be successful, to prevent a lot of money from becoming a little."**

There's nothing wrong with speculation, assuming you're doing so with money you can afford to lose. Younger people can usually afford to speculate and take greater risks since they're typically employed and have time on their side to hopefully recover from losses. The stock market makes a great home for this purpose. But people approaching retirement, needing the money to last 20 years or more, rarely can entertain such risk.

In his 1949 book *The Intelligent Investor,* Benjamin Graham argued that the single most unintelligent thing you could do is speculate when you think you are investing. To manage speculative exposure he advised, "put aside a portion—the smaller the better—of your capital in a separate fund for this purpose. Never add more money to this account. Never mingle your speculative and investment operations in the same account, nor in any part of your thinking."[30]

If we define investing as the effort to prevent a lot of money from becoming a little, retirees would be wise to measure their exposure to the stock market. **Even the most prolific investor of our era, the great Warren Buffet, boiled down the key to success to two simple rules: "Rule No. 1: Never lose money. Rule No. 2: Don't forget rule No. 1"!**

Mutual Funds — When you invest in mutual funds, you turn responsibility for choosing your stocks and bonds to a person, a team of professionals or a computer algorithm. You also gain the benefits of economies of scale, as your dollars are commingled with those from other investors, giving the collective greater flexibility, buying power and diversification. Thousands of mutual funds exist with wildly different objectives. They are far and away the most commonly used tools for retirement, with more than $74 trillion invested worldwide.[31]

Their main selling point is that funds offer expertise and proactive management. In theory, downside risk is somewhat reduced because your mutual fund invests in a wide range of stocks or bonds—it's diversified. But this service and convenience comes at a cost. Mutual funds impose fees, some of which can be hidden or difficult to calculate. These fees matter and, as we'll discover in Chapter 7, they aren't always justified.

Bonds — A bond is an "IOU". When somebody wants to borrow money and someone else has funds available to lend, they'll engage in an exchange where the lender expects their borrowed funds to

---

[30] Jason Zweig. JasonZweig.com. Dec. 9, 2016. "What's Speculating? What's Investing? Some of the Wisest Investors Weigh In." http://jasonzweig.com/whats-speculating-whats-investing-some-of-the-wisest-investors-weigh-in/.

[31] Financial Times. https://www.ft.com/content/5a395bb4-24a6-11e5-9c4e-a775d2b173ca

be returned with interest. Companies, state and local governments, and governmental entities like turnpike authorities and school districts are the most common bond issuers, as they have the largest appetite for borrowed funds.

The value of a bond is primarily driven by its quality, maturity and interest rate.

Quality refers to the likelihood that borrowed funds will be repaid. For instance, if I lend money to the city of Boston, I'm feeling confident that I'll get my money back with interest. I might not have the same confidence in lending to the city of Detroit, given their financial struggles.

Bond maturity tells you how soon you'll be repaid. Short-term bonds mature in five years or less. Long-term bonds can mature in 10, 20, 30 years or longer.

The biggest factor for many is the interest rate, the reward for lending your money. Interest rates are primarily influenced by the Federal Reserve Board (the Fed), which meets just eight times a year and rarely makes dramatic changes. The Fed has only moved rates three times since the financial crisis of 2008. [32]

Bonds and bond mutual funds have a reputation for being less volatile and hence are often thought to be less risky than stocks. Perhaps you've been advised to sequentially shift your portfolio away from stocks in favor of bonds as retirement approaches. The mutual fund industry has built a fleet of target-date mutual funds that do just that automatically for investors. However, the reputation of bonds being a bastion of safety is deceptive because it's short-sighted. It's all about those interest rates, baby!

This is best explained with an example:

---

[32] Binyamin Appelbaum. New York Times. March 15, 2017. "Fed Raises Interest Rates for Third Time Since Financial Crisis. https://www.nytimes.com/2017/03/15/business/economy/fed-interest-rates-yellen.html.

Back to the Future: Imagine going back in time to 1980. You buy a bond with interest tied to the prime rate — 15 percent. At that time, you would have thought nothing of a 15 percent interest rate, but by today's standards, what an investment!

Ten years pass and you find yourself in need of funds. Maybe you're buying a car, going on vacation or remodeling the house. You decide to cover your expenses by selling that old bond. You visit a broker and put the bond on the market for sale. By 1990 the prime rate had dropped to 9 percent. Any investor could buy a newly issued bond paying 9 percent or buy yours paying 15 percent. It's a no-brainer; your bond would sell immediately. But you're no fool; you know your bond is valuable. So, you demand a premium — a little extra to be paid by the buyer to reflect your bond's attractiveness.

This illustrates that when interest rates go down, bond prices go up. Folks retiring one generation ago had a great experience with their bond investments. Not only did they lock in phenomenal interest rates, but they also watched their bonds become more valuable as interest rates dropped. In part, the declining interest rate environment experienced during the past 30 years helped build the rock steady reputation that bonds still enjoy.

Let's fast forward and go through the same example using present day numbers. Interest rates have been at historic lows for a decade. But retirement is close and concerns for risk are high. Working out of the same worn playbook, you begin shifting out of stocks and buy into bonds with the prime rate at just 4 percent. But with interest rates just now climbing out from record lows, there's nowhere for rates to go but up.

Another 10 years pass; it's now 2027. You need another car, vacation or remodel. You go back to the broker. This time nobody is buying; not at first. Perhaps the prime rate has risen to 6 percent. An investor can buy a new bond paying 6 percent or your old bond, bought in 2017, paying 4 percent. Why would they purchase your bond? They wouldn't. Not unless you discounted your bond enough to put it on par with the more attractive options. In other words, you might not recover the original investment. **This illustrates that when interest rates go up, bond prices tend to go down.**

Our story cautions that bonds will probably not be the mainstay for conservative retirement savings that they once were, perhaps for an entire generation. Bonds still have a role in financial planning; but should be approached with guidance from your financial advisor.

Wall Street Wrap-up — Before we leave Wall Street let's review. Stocks, bonds and mutual funds offer GROWTH, but at the expense of PROTECTION. You'll have CONTROL over investment direction and withdrawals subject only to IRS guidelines or self-imposed investment restrictions. But, if risk to your hard-earned savings causes you to lose sleep, it may be time to visit another drawer in the toolbox.

Banks

So, you don't want to risk losing all your money. Then march down to America's favorite financial institution, your local bank! It provides principal protection that's guaranteed, up to a certain amount, by the Federal Deposit Insurance Corporation (FDIC).

Banks are lending institutions and profit off the interest earned on loans. They use your money to make their money, sharing a little bit of the interest with you as reward. Problem is, with interest rates so low, there's not much reward circulating these days and banks have gotten about as stingy as it gets.

Glory days: Do you remember getting those little postcards in the mail years ago featuring the orange bouncing ball? Unbound from the overhead associated with traditional brick-and-mortar institutions, the online banking division of ING had some of the best interest rates around. I distinctly remember getting north of 5% on a checking account! We used to help more conservatively minded clients position part of their nest eggs in these insured, yet rewarding bank products. These days, most people do their banking at interest rates starting with a decimal point.

Checking/Savings — Even the most clueless investor knows the deal. Cash parked in a bank savings or checking account is insured, but in this current low-interest environment your funds will earn a pittance.

CDs — A certificate of deposit will usually pay higher interest in exchange for a time commitment. Be mindful of your liquidity needs. If you ask the bank to return your funds in year two of a five-year commitment, they'll oblige, but not without extracting a penalty for early withdrawal. Five-year CD rates are finally approaching 2 percent after the last Fed rate hike.

Are low interest rates a problem? You better believe it! A return of 2 percent means you're losing money on an inflation-adjusted basis. While your principal might remain intact, out in the real world, the cost of commonly purchased goods and services is increasing by at least 3 percent annually on average.[33] Your "protected" dollars are losing purchasing power!

Banking Summary — The strengths and weaknesses should be clear. Banks offer PROTECTION and substantial CONTROL but not much in the way of GROWTH. Until interest rates substantially improve, the bank is typically good for short- and intermediate-term liquidity but not much else.

Insurance Companies

Wouldn't it be great if it were possible to earn an inflation-fighting interest rate but keep the principal protected at the same time? Insurance companies believe they have your answer. You want PROTECTION *and* GROWTH? Buy an annuity! But let's look before we leap.

---

[33] Tim McMahon. InflationData.com. April 1, 2014. "Long Term U.S. Inflation." https://inflationdata.com/inflation/inflation_rate/long_term_inflation.asp.

Another Visit to the Past

I can hardly contain my excitement; we have an opportunity for another history lesson! It would serve us well to explore annuities in greater detail. Annuities tend to be relatively new concepts for people approaching retirement; after all, there's little need for an annuity when you're 20, 30 or 40 years old. As a result, annuities generate more misinformation, aggressive sales practices and trepidation than any other financial solution, in my experience.

Relax. Annuities are just another tool, but are defined by their unique contractual design. You're probably more familiar with them than you think. I'd venture to say that nearly every American will benefit from an annuity during their retirement whether they're aware of it or not.

In a previous chapter, we learned the Romans introduced the pension to protect the interests of the state and its military veterans. The concept was immensely popular and soon ordinary Roman citizens were clamoring for a civilian version.

A Roman judge, Gnaeus Domitius Annius Ulpianus, is credited with paving the way. He created some of the first *annuae,* which is Latin for annual stipend. Citizens could create a contract with the empire that would guarantee them annual payments for life, or a specified period, in exchange for a lump sum payment. Ulpianus also created some of the first actuarial tables, used to determine a participant's benefits based on their payment, age and time horizon.

The popularity of the *annuae* is easy to understand. In any era, once people reach a certain age, they tend to prize income over speculation. So, an *annua,* similar to an annuity, addresses this issue by guaranteeing income or principal for a specified period of time, usually for life.

As with all financial products there was a catch. When a participant died, their payments were kept by the *annua* and redistributed to the others. This was by design. These anticipated redistributions, known as mortality credits, allowed participants to receive much higher annual payments than they could otherwise generate on their own. The premature death of one participant was a boon to others in the pool. But, as a result, the investor's family got nothing. Such was the risk.

Thank goodness, after over two millennia, we've outgrown the limitations of this old Roman system. Or have we?

Consider that Social Security and corporate pensions are little different from Roman *annuae*. Today, instead of a lump sum payment, we make systematic payments over time into a common pool to receive guaranteed income later in life. While most modern annuities feature spousal benefits with limitations, they provide nothing for extended family members. Think about it—what do the kids get when you pass away? When it comes to Social Security and pensions, the answer is usually nothing.

Immediate and Deferred Annuities — Roman *annuae* still exist today by other names: there are immediate and deferred annuities. The difference between the two is when you start receiving the income—immediately or at a specified point in the future.

When you retire, income becomes a paramount concern. Immediate and deferred annuities, being able to take advantage of pooling mortality credits, offer some of the highest guaranteed lifetime payouts available—if you're willing to turn a sum of money into a stream of income. Annuities can be very helpful when Social Security and pensions won't cover all the bills and can be leveraged to create lifetime income with greater certainty than a risk-oriented market portfolio.

But taking the income stream is often a permanent decision – it's unlikely you'll be allowed access to your lump sum in the event of an emergency. And for estate planning purposes, it's important to note that immediate and deferred annuities can significantly limit or eliminate the possibility that anything will be left over for heirs or dependents. That can be a big risk, depending on your legacy goals—especially for people who die before substantially benefiting from their contract.

Modern Variations

An annuity can responsibly make guarantees, as accounts are contractual, backed by the strength of the issuing insurance company.

In recent decades, as retirement has evolved, the insurance industry has introduced several modern variations of the annuity to appeal to different segments of the retirement population, given the different attitudes people have related to income, risk and reward.

Fixed Annuities – These annuities were designed to give consumers a predictable interest rate for a fixed duration of time. For instance, the highest-paying 5-year fixed annuity, offered through an A-rated insurance company, is paying just north of 3 percent in 2017.

Annuities often allow annual penalty-free withdrawals to help address short-term liquidity needs. Most insurance companies allow consumers to withdraw up to 10 percent of their annuity's accumulated value annually, during the maturity period, free of penalty. While this is a welcome feature, the withdrawal is subject to income taxes, and potentially an additional penalty if you are under age 59 ½. Therefore, annuities should still be considered relatively illiquid during their maturity periods. It's precisely for this reason you should never invest all your money in an annuity.

> **Locked Up?** A common response to the 10 percent withdrawal limitation is, "I don't want to lock up my money." Nobody does. But don't kid yourself; your retirement money is already locked up. Most people have their retirement savings in 401(k)s and IRAs. After age 59 ½, you can take withdrawals whenever you'd like, but 100 percent of the distribution is taxable as ordinary income. Withdrawing more than 10 percent in any given year during retirement risks the invitation of a substantial tax bill.

> Furthermore, your retirement nest egg must be capable of lasting 20 years or more. Too many withdrawals of 10 percent or more would risk your nest egg depleting too quickly. If anything, a 10 percent withdrawal limitation assists with enforcing the discipline you should already be exercising in retirement.

Variable Annuities — Not happy with 3 percent growth? The variable annuity was created to achieve higher rates of return. On their surface, they share some characteristics of a 401(k) plan. You're given a list of investment options, called subaccounts, among which you can deploy your investment dollars. What makes the variable annuity unique is that you can couple market exposure with guarantees. Investing is a risky proposition, so having some protection would make sense as retirement nears. For example, you might be able to guarantee that your principal is preserved regardless of market performance, that a minimum death benefit will be provided to your beneficiaries or even guarantee income for life regardless of investment performance or fund exhaustion.

Sounds great! But every time you elect to guarantee this or guarantee that you might hear a loud *ka-ching!* Those protections certainly are not free. Variable annuities own the somewhat dubious distinction of being one of the more expensive tools in the financial toolbox.

There's a fee for the investment options, an insurance company charge (called mortality and expense), administrative charges and then fees for the optional guarantees (called riders). It's not unusual for a variable annuity to cost between 3-6 percent annually! Don't forget the surrender penalties applied for withdrawals taken in excess of the 10 percent annual withdrawal allowance during the maturity period.

The variable annuity is one of the most commonly marketed financial vehicles by some advisors. Those underlying fees often translate into big commissions for the solicitor. This is just another reason it's important to work with a fiduciary, so you can be confident that recommendations are best for you above all else.

"Never buy an annuity!" is engrained in many minds of today's retirees. This seems silly given that people love their pensions and Social Security checks, which offer payments that resemble an annuity. But there are many reasons that annuities have developed a bad reputation. Annuities are often accused of being complicated and expensive. Often, the variable annuity is at the root of these concerns. They can be difficult to justify for retirement purposes given the alternatives.

Now for the flip side. Some of you may want to defer taxes on investment portfolios or have the risk appetite to generate the returns necessary to offset those variable annuity fees. For you, variable annuities may make a good fit. It's also important to note that an additional-cost rider, not annuitization, is what often guarantees the income provided by variable annuities, so any leftover funds do pass to beneficiaries.

Fixed Indexed Annuities — These products are the newest addition to the annuity lineup. Introduced in 1995, a fixed indexed annuity combines some of the benefits of its fixed and variable counterparts: you can earn interest based on a market index, with guarantees to your principal. Interest is based on a selected market index coupled with constraints known as the *floor, cap, spread* and/or *participation rate.*

Let's say the S&P 500 is the index used to determine credited interest, with a 6 percent cap and a 0 percent floor. What happens if the market goes up 10 percent? You'd earn 6 percent, because the cap represents your upper boundary. Should the market crash, dropping 30 percent, you would lose nothing. The floor, representing the lower boundary, protects your principal and your previous interest credits, which are locked in each year. The indexed annuity is like a ratchet, only moving in one direction, making it opportunistic in good times and defensive in bad.

When you purchase a fixed indexed annuity, your money is never actually invested in the underlying index. The index is only used as a measure for determining your interest. This is a product without market risk, capable of achieving better interest rates than some other protection-oriented financial solutions. As described, sounds too good to be true, right?

Remember, no tool is perfect. While fixed indexed annuities can have the potential to earn competitive interest rates, you don't reap other ancillary benefits of traditional investing like receiving dividends. Fixed indexed annuities are also subject to the same liquidity limitations as fixed and variable annuities. Annual penalty-free withdrawals are typically limited to 10 percent of the annuity's present value during the maturity period.

Annuity Roundup — The era of banks and bonds dominating the realm of "protected" retirement investments is long past. Annuities can offer guaranteed income, interest rates or principal protection, all of which are very attractive in this difficult, volatile and low-interest rate environment.

Annuities provide PROTECTION and limited GROWTH potential, but at the expense of complete CONTROL. Remember, withdrawals from most annuities will be limited to 10 percent per year during their maturity periods. And in the case of immediate or deferred annuities, CONTROL of your funds may be forfeited at death.

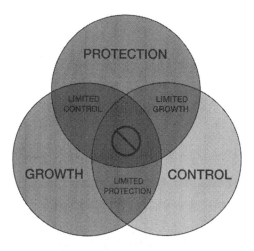

Finding Harmony

An interesting concept, observed repeatedly throughout history by many cultures and religions, is belief that the most sacred ideas have a three-fold nature. The central mystery of the Catholic faith holds that there is but one God manifested by three wholly distinct entities: the Father, the Son and the Holy Spirit. The Jewish Kabbalah speaks of the three in "All That Is" — Nothingness, Wisdom and Understanding. Buddhists meditate on the triadic nature of self: Mind, Body and Soul.

The concept of three elements working in harmony has been explored throughout the ages but may be most beautifully symbolized by the Celtic knot or triquetra. Any fan of rock and roll or tattoo art knows it well:

Applying this philosophy to the financial toolbox within the constraints of growth, protection and control yields a similar looking result:

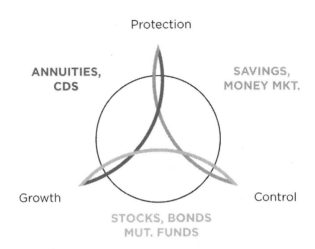

Protection

ANNUITIES, CDS

SAVINGS, MONEY MKT.

Growth

Control

STOCKS, BONDS MUT. FUNDS

Wall Street products dominate the retirement landscape. The growth potential of these vehicles is without question an effective tool for combating inflation. But how Wall Street will perform in the future is uncertain, making it a suspect choice for the primary source of income when you retire.

Keeping money in the bank allows us immediate access to funds in case of emergency or an unexpected expense with few limitations. The problem is that bank accounts currently offer laughable rates of interest.

Annuities offered by insurance companies can be a great place to protect some of your money while still allowing opportunity for growth, resulting in a stable source of income. But anticipated withdrawals must be taken sequentially as to not run afoul of penalty.

Unfortunately, when deciding how to allocate the retirement nest egg, many retirees survey the financial toolbox

and ask the *wrong* question. They'll consult Google, their accountant or maybe a rich uncle and inquire, "Where's the best place to put my money?

It might be better to direct that question to your local fortune teller. It sure would be easy to make decisions with your money if you knew exactly how markets, interest rates and the global economy were to perform in the short and long term! But, given that nobody can predict the future, why do we engage in endless speculation about the "best" place to put your money when any singular tool has unique risks that might be disastrous in the wrong circumstances?

Call it old fashioned or overly-simplistic, but I believe you shouldn't put all your eggs in one basket. As an advisor, I've spent countless hours ruminating on the right tools to use in helping clients navigate retirement and an uncertain future. Time and experience have taught me that the best plans do not rest on any one concept or strategy but rather on the inclusion of all that the financial industry can offer. In doing so, I find that the respective STRENGTHS of these strategies serve to overcome their individual WEAKNESSES.

I don't claim that there's any spiritual significance in combining these tools, but there's a certain beauty in this approach. I believe it's the best way to go when facing an uncertain future.

It's time to focus on how we can use these tools to build the plan of your dreams. Let's get started.

CHAPTER FIVE

Income

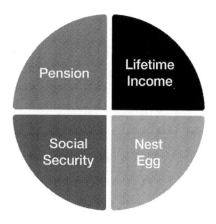

"It is better to have a permanent income than to be fascinating."
—Oscar Wilde

"A large income is the best recipe for happiness I ever heard of."
—Jane Austen

You've been doing it for years. Working. Saving. Taking risks. Slowly but surely, your nest egg has grown to where it stands to-day. Whatever the dollar value of your retirement savings, it represents years of hard work and sacrifice. Think about all the vacations you could have taken, all the fancy gadgets, jewelry and clothes you could have purchased, all the wild nights on the town passed by to build that nest egg.

But, unlike many Americans, you saved in the hope of having a meaningful and fulfilling retirement; a retirement where you can not only cover the bills, but more importantly—*enjoy life.*

One of my favorite movies is *Braveheart.* There's a scene where a stoic William Wallace, defiant in the face of his own impending execution, attempts to reassure the French princess by saying, "Every man dies. Not every man really lives."

Wallace's wise words did little to comfort the infatuated princess, but they have always resonated when I'm helping people design their retirement plans. Every person can retire, but not everyone enjoys a retirement worth having. My words might not be as poetic as those of the old Scot, but hopefully you get the gist.

That nest egg needs to be prudently leveraged so you can enjoy your current lifestyle for the rest of your life. Since you're reading this book, my guess is that the missing piece is a plan to make that happen. In this chapter, I'm going to outline the steps I believe you'll need to take to make that plan a reality.

The good news is that it's not rocket science. The tools to deliver your desired outcome are readily available. So, what's the key to maintaining that lifestyle you so enjoy? The answer is *income.*

We've always been told to measure our progress toward retirement by tallying the value of our assets. But assets are *not* income. Your house is an asset, probably one of your biggest, but its value is not easily exchanged to buy groceries or an all-inclusive vacation package. Your 401(k) is certainly an asset, but you can't use it for retirement purposes until you convert it to cash.

A client was recently telling me how much money he had made in Apple stock after a nice little run in the market. I patiently reminded him he hadn't made anything—not yet. At first, he was perplexed; the value of his stock was nearly 50 percent greater than what he had paid for it. I calmly explained that no market gains or losses are real until the asset is turned into cash. Until that happens, the Apple stock could continue to skyrocket or plummet the other way. Nothing is officially gained or lost until the cold hard cash is in your hand.

You need to make one very important leap in your thinking. Giving your retirement plan liftoff is going to require that you adopt an income-oriented mindset. Assets are great, but as far as retirement planning is concerned INCOME IS KING.

Sure Thing or a Maybe?

We have to get this right; nobody wants to risk running out of money in retirement. That's why it's so important to plan for retirement with an income-oriented mindset. Assets can be depleted, but income, if designed correctly, can last a lifetime.

Retirees love income. Think about it. Have you ever heard anyone say they dislike their pensions or Social Security? I've conducted hundreds of seminars and I always have fun with the pensioners in the room. I like to ask if they'd be interested in trading in their pensions for a 401(k). The answer is always a resounding "NO!" Pensioners love their guaranteed income. Assuming the employer will honor its promise to pay - it's a sure thing. Incidentally, I *do* have some advice for pensioners, which some may find surprising, later in this chapter.

The rest of us are stuck with maybes. Our 401(k)s and IRAs *might* be able to serve as a source of lifetime income, but if we live long enough or if the market doesn't cooperate at the wrong times we run the risk of running out of money.

Is it any wonder that a recent survey conducted by the Transamerica Center for Retirement Studies found that the greatest concern for 51 percent of Americans aged 50 and older was running out of money in retirement?[34] Luckily, as you'll learn here, it's possible to convert those 401(k)s and IRAs into a lifetime income.

Ask yourself a very important question: do you want to build your retirement plan primarily with sure things or maybes? If you're like me, you want the certainty of a sure thing.

Budget

Before we go any further, you need to calculate your future income needs. This part isn't difficult; there's no need to overcomplicate things. If you don't already have a budget, you should create one. Begin with a list of everything you currently spend money on each month.

Let's consider staples. These are things you spend money on every single month. Real estate taxes, groceries, utilities and insurance—your basic needs. Don't forget to account for items that may change depending on the season or time of year. Heating oil and home maintenance are great examples of routine expenses that don't appear month-to-month.

Next, you'll need to estimate your discretionary items. These are your wants. Vacations, hobbies, gifts for family members, nights on the town, etc. Make sure you budget enough in this area so you can build a plan that allows you to enjoy life to its fullest!

Be careful to identify current commitments that you anticipate going away before or during retirement. I call these the drop-off items. For example, the systematic savings directed toward your 401(k) plan will end when you leave your employer. Other common budget items that fall off at some point include the mortgage, car

---

[34] TransAmerica Center for Retirement Studies. August 2016. "Perspectives on Retirement: Baby Boomers, Generation X, and Millennials." https://www.transamericacenter.org/docs/default-source/retirement-survey-of-workers/tcrs2016_sr_perspectives_on_retirement_baby_boomers_genx_millennials.pdf.

payments or expenses associated with children such as college tuition.

Tally up your needs and wants; make allowances for the drop-off items and *voilà* you have a target for the monthly income you'll need to support a comfortable retirement! But is it enough? I always ask clients if the product of our budgeting exercise is on target. To no surprise, everybody usually wants a little more for extra cushion or funny money. I'd recommend you think about rounding up to the nearest thousand and consider adding another 10-20 percent beyond that. The extra income can provide a lot of joy and provides flexibility for the unexpected. You deserve that.

Write your number down. Our sole objective is to make sure we can consistently deliver enough income to cover this anticipated monthly retirement budget.

If you need help getting organized, you can start with the following basic monthly expense chart.

	Your Monthly Expenses (aka: Budget)					
Housing	Rent/mortgage		*Transportation*	Public transit	
	Home insurance			Gas	
	Utilities			Parking/tolls	
	Internet/cable			Maintenance	
	Phones			Insurance	
	Taxes			Loan payments	
	Household supplies			Other	
	Total	$		**Total**	$
Food	Groceries		*Personal*	Child care	
	Meals out			Gifts	
	Other			Clothes/shoes	
	Total	$		Laundry	
Health	Medicine			Donations	
	Insurance			Entertainment	
	Out-of-pocket			Beauty care	
	Other			Other	
	Total	$		**Total**	$
Finance	Financial professional		*Other*	School costs	
	Bank fees			Credit cards	
	Other fees or expenses			Savings	
	Total	$		**Total**	$
				Grand Total	$

Tying in Social Security

It's time to revisit our old friend Social Security. We've discussed the federal program at length, covering its history and future. But now it's time to put it to work for your situation.

The rules governing Social Security are vast and nuanced. There are special provisions covering the unique needs of widows, divorcees and the disabled. We'll leave the exploration of every nook and cranny of the program to separate analyses. For our purposes, I only want to cover the most basic concepts; the things you absolutely need to know and the pitfalls you'll want to avoid.

There's a lot at stake here. For most people, Social Security is their largest retirement asset. I know that statement may come as a shock but it's true. We take this for granted because we mistakenly overvalue assets over income. The big numbers you see on your investment statements are more impressive looking than the small three or four figure monthly benefit you see on your Social Security projection. But when you do the math a different picture emerges.

Adding it up: Assume you're married and that you and your spouse are each entitled to full retirement age benefits of $2,000 per month. That's a combined total of $4,000 per month or $48,000 per year. If you live just 10 years, you'll collect $480,000 from the Social Security administration. Live 20 years and you'll collect $960,000. Make it 25 years, closer to average life expectancy, and you'll collect a whopping $1,200,000. That's without even factoring in cost-of-living adjustments!

The catch is you must live long enough and avoid all the penalties to get as much of that benefit as possible. The difference between collecting the right way or the wrong way could cost you hundreds of thousands of dollars.

Collecting Early — Most Americans begin collecting Social Security at age 62,[35] primarily because they want the money and they want it NOW. But unless you're desperate for additional funds this is often a mistake.

Collecting before full retirement age (FRA) subjects your benefit to actuarial reductions. Your benefit is considered fully vested when you reach FRA, which for most people is either 66 or 67, depending on the year in which you were born.

Age To Receive Full Social Security Benefits* *(Called "full retirement age" or "normal retirement age.")*	
Year of Birth*	**FRA**
1937 or earlier	65
1938	65 and 2 months
1939	65 and 4 months
1940	65 and 6 months
1941	65 and 8 months
1942	65 and 10 months
1943--1954	66
1955	66 and 2 months
1956	66 and 4 months
1957	66 and 6 months
1958	66 and 8 months
1959	66 and 10 months
1960 and later	67

If you were born on January 1st of any year you should refer to the previous year. (If you were born on the 1st of the month, we figure your benefit (and your full retirement age) as if your birthday was in the previous month.)

---

[35] Alicia H. Munnell and Anqi Chen. Center for Retirement Research at Boston College. May 2015. "Trends in Social Security Claiming." http://crr.bc.edu/briefs/trends-in-social-security-claiming/.

If you begin collecting your Social Security benefits prior to reaching your FRA, you'll experience a benefit reduction. The severity of the reduction is dependent on how far in advance of your FRA that you begin benefits. This illustration demonstrates the impact of these reductions.

Social Security: Benefits of Delayed withdrawal

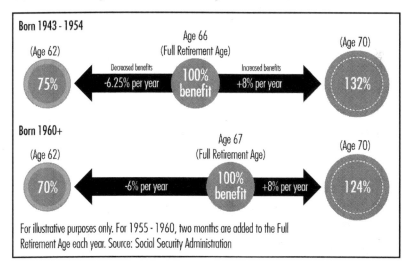

Those collecting at age 62 are potentially forfeiting 30 percent or more of their lifetime benefit! That's a difference of thousands of dollars over the course of an average life expectancy.

The pain doesn't stop there. The Social Security administration assesses a separate work-related penalty for those who collect benefits *and* continue to work prior to FRA. Here's how it works: after FRA you can collect and work to your heart's content without penalty. But as of 2017, if you collect prior to FRA, you're only allowed to earn work-related compensation of $16,920 without consequence. For every two dollars you earn beyond this limit, you'll forfeit one dollar of Social Security.

In the year you reach FRA, the exempted amount of income increases to $44,880 and the penalty becomes a one dollar loss for every three dollars earned beyond the limit. It's only the compensation earned in the months prior to your birthday that count against you. Confused by all the rules and calculations? You're not alone!

> **Work-related penalty**: Assume you begin collecting Social Security at age 64 while continuing to earn $50,000 from your employer. Your income puts you $33,080 beyond the limit ($50,000 - $16,920 = $33,080). Your penalty is $1 for every $2 earned beyond the limit, so you'll forfeit $16,540 ($33,080 ÷ 2 = $16,540). What a waste!

The takeaway is that the Social Security administration is heavily discouraging you from collecting early. The dollars are certainly yours for the taking, but you'll only get a fraction when you start the clock early.

Good Things Come to Those Who Wait — Not everything is bad news when it comes to Social Security. You also get rewarded for every year beyond FRA that benefits are deferred. These are known as delayed retirement credits and they help grow your FRA by an additional 8 percent per year until you reach age 70!

This credit is about as generous as it gets. In 2017, there aren't too many places you can get an 8 percent increase on any kind of retirement savings or benefit. If you like your job or just plan on working a little longer, know that you can reap the benefits of these increases.

> **Planning tip**: When possible and appropriate for their situation, I encourage married couples to have one spouse take full advantage of delayed retirement credits by waiting until age 70 to collect. When one spouse passes away, the survivor gets to keep the larger of the two benefits. If the higher-earning spouse delays collecting benefits until 70 it's guaranteed that the remaining spouse get the largest survivor benefit possible! Of course, every situation is unique; our planning process can help you determine if this strategy would work well for your situation.

Break-Even Analysis — Some watercooler experts will maintain that delayed credits aren't worth it. They'll argue that it's better to receive smaller payments for a longer period, than larger payments for a shorter period. They might even spice their analysis with a dose of fearmongering or misinformation—*Social Security is ending any moment, collect while you still can and get grandfathered benefits before things change!*

By and large, I believe they're wrong. This may come as a surprise, given the grim forecast we painted for Social Security in an earlier chapter. But nobody can predict how and when Social Security will change, who will be affected and under what circumstances. We can only make decisions based on the rules as they exist today; speculation is just a tail chasing exercise. To judge whether it makes sense to collect before or after FRA, we simply look to break-even analysis.

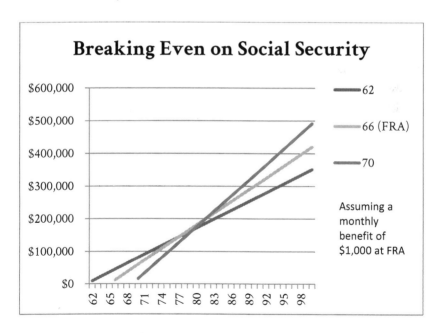

All things being equal, the people who collect benefits early certainly get a head start on everyone else; but the rest of the pack catches up and forever leaves the early birds behind around age 80. And, since most Americans are expected to live well beyond age 80, the watercooler advice doesn't always hold. Considering that health care costs and taxes are expected to rise in the future, you better think twice before collecting benefits too soon.

There are, of course, exceptions. If you believe that you might have a shorter than average life expectancy or if there's compelling need for additional income in the short-term, then it may be in your best interest to take benefits early.

What's at Stake? — Early in this chapter we used an example of a married couple eligible to collect a combined $4,000 per month at FRA. Let's assume that future cost-of-living adjustments average 1.5 percent per year and that our imaginary couple makes it to age 90.

If they start collecting at age 62, given the actuarial deductions, they'll collect cumulative benefits of $1,239,168. If they instead start Social Security at FRA, they'll collect a total of $1,458,792. And if they max out at age 70, their lifetime total will eclipse $1,650,432. That's right, for our prototype couple the difference between collecting the most and the least is nearly half a million dollars!

Social Security – Timing Decisions				
Age Benefits Start	Monthly Amount	Lifetime Benefits	$ Difference	% Difference
62	$1,508	$1,239,168	-	-
66	$2,123	$1,458,792	$219,624	18%
70	$2,974	$1,650,432	$411,264	33%

That's real money that could be used for incredible vacations or putting a grandchild through college. The analysis didn't even factor in all the various other ways that you might collect less from Social Security due to taxes, penalties and other pitfalls.

The shame is that people leave money on the table because they are not being properly educated or taking the time to inform themselves about their options. The Social Security administration is prohibited from providing financial advice, but we are counting on them to give us accurate information. Unfortunately, that's not always the case.

The Government Accountability Office (GAO) conducted a review of the Social Security claims process in various offices throughout the country and found "claimants were not consistently provided key information that people may need to make well-informed decisions." Among Social Security staff the study found "widespread misunderstanding about whether spousal benefits are available, how monthly benefits are determined and how the retirement earnings test works." [36]

A close inspection conducted by a Forbes contributor found that Social Security even has inaccurate information on its own *website*. The scathing assessment advised that claimants, "not ask Social Security anything ... do not read anything on their website and, for that matter, do not use their online tools, which ... cannot even provide correct benefit estimates." Retirees are advised to use reliable Social Security software output to determine the best course of action. "Don't take no for an answer. As a group, Social Security staff is not to be trusted, so you literally need to shop around to find someone who actually knows the rules." [37]

While pessimistic, I believe the advice is sound. There's simply too much at stake to let potential incompetency affect the corner-

---

[36] U.S. Government Accountability Office. Sept. 14, 2016. "Social Security: Improvements to Claims Process Could Help People Make Better Informed Decisions About Retirement Benefits." http://www.gao.gov/products/GAO-16-786.

[37] Laurence Kotlikoff. Forbes. Feb. 7, 2017. "Social Security Can't Even Get Its FAQs Right." https://www.forbes.com/sites/kotlikoff/2017/02/07/social-security-cant-even-get-its-faqs-right/#5171d4737edc.

stone of your lifetime retirement income. The output from the Social Security software we use in our office is available to anyone who asks, free of charge or commitment.

Do your homework. Turning on Social Security isn't like flicking on a light switch. There's real money — BIG money at stake.

Interested in knowing the options to collect Social Security for your specific situation? Visit our website to request your complimentary Social Security Analysis:

www.arcadia.financial/socialsecurityanalysis

Pensions

If you don't have a pension, you can safely skip this section. If you do have a pension, the generic advice provided here may or may not apply; each pension is highly individualized. Some offer lump sum payouts, survivor benefits or enhanced benefits, while others do not. What you should do regarding your own pension is subject to individual analysis. That said, there are a couple of general tips I can share.

Do your homework — Subject your pension to the same rigorous analysis that you would Social Security. Since each pension is unique, you'll need to collect pertinent information directly from your employer regarding how the calculation is performed; the rewards and penalties based on age of withdrawal, what spousal protections are provided, if lump sum withdrawal is available, etc. Human resources and pension management staff are, in my experience, both notoriously understaffed and slow to respond to requests so this is a process best started *years* in advance of retirement.

Mayday Mayday Mayday — Next, be mindful of the *sustainability* of your pension. As discussed earlier, economists believe that pensions, both private and public, may be underfunded to the tune of billions or even trillions of dollars.

Pension problems: Think your pension couldn't possibly be stripped away or reduced? Think again. Ask a former employee of Bethlehem Steel or Polaroid what all the promises their companies made amounted to at the end of the day: $0. In fairness, outright pension dissolution is rare. But frozen and reduced pensions are common. The following is a partial list of well-known companies that have drastically reduced pension benefits in recent years: Verizon, IBM, General Motors, Coca-Cola, DuPont, Michelin, Citigroup, 3M, Boeing, Saks, Anheuser-Busch, Sunoco, Kraft Foods, Caterpillar, Allstate and Lockheed Martin.[38] The common thread is that these companies are all large enough to have been once considered benefit-reduction proof.

Pensions in distress will continue to dominate the news for years to come. The city of Dallas is making headlines as its police and firefighters are pulling lump sum benefits in droves from a chronically underfunded plan. Millions of baby boomers are at risk of falling victim to mismanagement and ludicrous benefit-crediting methodologies.

Elsewhere in the news, the New York Teamsters Road Carriers Local 707 Pension Fund has claim to the unfortunate distinction of being the nation's first pension to run out of money entirely. The plan is now in Pension Benefits Guaranty Corporation receivership with recipients receiving benefits, albeit at substantially reduced rates.[39]

For years, there were federal protections in place to help prevent pensions from being cut. Few pensioners are aware that this changed in December 2014 when Congress quietly

---

[38] Pension Rights Center. June 27, 2017. "Companies That Have Changed Their Defined Benefit Pension Plans." http://www.pensionrights.org/publications/factsheet/companies-have-changed-their-defined-benefit-pension-plans.

[39] Ginger Adams Otis. Daily News. Feb. 26, 2017. "Drained Pension Fund Has Retired New York Union Workers Pinching Pennies to Survive, as Doom Looms for Reserves Across U.S." http://www.nydailynews.com/new-york/n-y-retirees-struggle-survive-pension-fund-bottoms-article-1.2982399.

inserted a provision into the $1.1 trillion government spending bill that allows multi-employer pension plans to cut benefits by as much as 69 percent so long as they are projected to run out of money within one or two decades.[40]

The Central States Pension Fund, servicing retirement benefits for Teamsters union truck drivers across Texas, Michigan, Wisconsin, Missouri, New York and Minnesota became the first plan in the nation to apply for approval to reduce benefits under the new law.[41] They probably won't be the last.

Here's a simple test to learn if your pension plan might be in danger of being reduced or changed. Take note of the single-life pension benefit at retirement age. Next, if possible, calculate how much income you could generate if you accepted a lump sum payout and invested the proceeds into a single-life annuity.

Is your pension paying substantially more than the annuity? If so, the pension may be in trouble. After all, insurance companies are in the business of paying sustainable lifetime income. Your employer providing the pension probably is not. The pension might be making promises that will prove difficult to keep. Other organizations will fall prey to corruption, political gamesmanship, poor management and other shenanigans. Be sure to ask for financials on the sustainability and solvency of the plan. A pension can provide financial confidence in retirement, but only if all the promises are honored.

I Will Survive! — Another item warranting scrutiny is your pension's survivor benefits. Most of the time, you'll be offered a

---

[40] Pension Rights Center. December 2014. "Summary of the Pension Cutback Provisions in the Multiemployer Pension Reform Act of 2014." http://www.pensionrights.org/issues/legislation/summary-pension-cutback-provisions-multiemployer-pension-reform-act-2014.

[41] Jonnelle Marte. The Washington Post. April 20, 2016. "One of the Nation's Largest Pension Funds Could Soon Cut Benefits for Retirees." https://www.washingtonpost.com/news/get-there/wp/2016/04/20/one-of-the-nations-largest-pension-funds-could-soon-cut-benefits-for-retirees/?utm_term=.4082d2e7c202.

large monthly pension with no continuance after your death. The alternative, depending on plan availability, is to collect a smaller monthly pension that can continue for the life of your spouse or to a non-spouse beneficiary for a limited period.

If you're married, it's a real gamble to turn down those survivor benefits. Most people want assurance that their loved ones will benefit from their pensions dollars in their absence.

But those survivor benefits aren't necessarily the best deal. Pension survivor benefits do not require underwriting. This means your employer will assume the risk of paying benefits beyond your death whether you're a triathlete or a chain-smoking bungee jumper. In other words, you're not being rewarded with richer benefits for being healthy as you would be with traditional life insurance.

Here's another great exercise to explore. It's called pension maximization using life insurance. Take the difference between the maximum single-life pension payout and the 100 percent joint-and-survivor benefit. We'll call that the premium. The test is to see if that premium could be used to replicate the same survivor benefits by buying a private life insurance policy.

Pension maximization with life insurance can offer some substantial benefits. If you outlive your spouse, you can simply cancel the life insurance and reap the benefits of having preserved the larger pension payout. Now, imagine if both you and your spouse are struck by an 18-wheeler. Who gets the pension benefits then? Typically, it's nobody. But if you owned life insurance, that benefit would stay in the family and pay something forward to your estate. Pension maximization with life insurance can be a great strategy for some, but is highly dependent on your plan options and life expectancy. Also, life insurance itself can be a complicated product, usually requiring medical—sometimes financial—underwriting. As with all financial products, it involves fees and charges, limitations and restrictions, and often a penalty for withdrawals. If you want to consider this option, be sure to work with a qualified professional who will help you understand all the important details of this approach.

Final Thoughts — Be sure to keep meticulous records on your plan, including summaries and projections. Ask to see the rules governing the plan so you understand how your benefit is calculated, how it coordinates with Social Security and what hoops you need to jump through to collect. Take nothing for granted when doing your homework.

Mind the Gap

Let's bring all we've learned together. Earlier I asked you to comb through your budget and come up with your number—the target amount of income you want to collect every month to have the retirement of your dreams. After tallying Social Security and pension benefits, how close are you to meeting your goal?

Don't be alarmed if you're not there yet. Social Security was originally designed to cover the most basic of living expenses: food, shelter and medical care. You won't be picking up a country club membership on the back of that benefit. Pensions can certainly get you a lot farther, but they're less common, less substantial and at-risk due to underfunding.

Monthly Budget – Social Security – Pensions = GAP

The difference between your number and the total of all sources of guaranteed retirement income is your GAP. We're putting that word in caps because filling your GAP is our primary objective—to make it such that your number is satisfied to the best possible extent, with limited risk of interruption or failure.

Remember, the greatest risk you have in retirement is longevity. And most GAP-filling resources present the potential risk of running dry. Whether your money is invested in IRAs,

401(k)s, CDs or other instruments, if you live long enough, if interest rates remain suppressed or if the market doesn't cooperate, there's a chance your plan could unravel.

This might be coming as a surprise, because for decades the financial industry has trumpeted that it's possible to address your GAP using a balanced, well-diversified portfolio of stocks and bonds. Because the market always delivers, right?

Here Be Dragons

A portfolio of stocks and bonds might be part of a well-balanced portfolio, but plenty of evidence shows that relying on one in isolation is probably a bad idea. Still, a pervasive number of financial planners and the American public believe that reliance solely on a risk-oriented portfolio is the right way to go when planning for retirement.

In Medieval times, creating accurate maps was difficult. Much of the world was still unexplored, measurement techniques were crude and map production was expensive. Whether by ignorance or superstition, these old maps are littered with all manner of beasts and serpents on the fringes of known territory. The message being *we don't exactly know what's out there — could be dragons!*

Maps today are far more accurate, including those we create for retirement, but there's still peril on the fringes. What happens if our well-laid plan doesn't work out? Running out of money in retirement might not be the same as being gobbled by a dragon, but they're both unpleasant outcomes! Why are so many people comfortable mapping out their financial futures on the back of risk-oriented investments?

The 4% Rule

Back in 1994, a financial planner in Southern California named William Bengen was vexed when a client asked how large his retirement nest egg needed to be to confidently retire. Bengen, an MIT graduate, began an exhaustive exercise in which he examined the performance of various portfolio allocations over rolling 30-year periods going back to 1926. His goal was to determine which allocation could deliver the most reliable inflation-adjusted income without risk of exhaustion.

His findings were published in the *Journal of Financial Planning,* in which he shared that a stock-tilted portfolio could reliably produce retirement income at a 4.5 percent withdrawal rate.[42] His conclusion was rounded down when reported by the financial media and the "4% rule" was officially born.

Both directly and indirectly this single research study has affected more retirement plans than perhaps any other. This is entirely understandable, it's simple to understand and seemingly easy to execute. Achieving a 4 percent withdrawal rate should be easy. After all, a portfolio of 60 percent stocks and 40 percent bonds has

---

[42] William P. Bengen. Journal of Financial Planning. October 1994. "Determining Withdrawal Rates Using Historical Data." http://www.retailinvestor.org/pdf/Bengen1.pdf.

averaged an annual return of 8.7 percent between 1926 and 2015.[43] The resulting consensus is that the market, while having its ups and downs, has historically delivered over time.

Too good to be true? — First, be wary of universal consensus. Didn't consensus tell us that Hillary Clinton would win in a landslide in 2016? Just because so-called experts agree on something doesn't mean they're right. People are great at being spectacularly wrong.

Second, *past performance is not indicative of future performance.* There's good reason that this disclosure is so universal. We've already covered how the past cannot guide us through what's sure to be an uncertain future. A future in which pillars of retirement planning, including Social Security, Medicare and pensions are in flux and will certainly change.

This country is facing *major* retirement planning problems that are going to require a great deal of work to solve. Implementing solutions and enduring the bumps they cause along the way may be so jarring as to upset even the most carefully laid plans.

No matter what market cheerleaders tell you, there is *no* historical track record of the market being the primary vehicle to carry an entire generation through retirement. Sure, the Greatest Generation dabbled in the market and used it for supplementary income. But they also had a solvent Social Security program and much better pensions. **It's baby boomers who are going to test whether the market is capable of being the primary supplier of lifetime income. How's it feel to be the guinea pig?**

If you're like me, you don't want to rely entirely on risk-oriented assets to provide for your financial future. I don't mind gambling in the market with some of my money; but only with what I can afford to lose. For the money I'm going to need, the money I'm going to

---

[43] Vanguard. "Vanguard Portfolio Allocation Models." https://personal.vanguard.com/us/insights/saving-investing/model-portfolio-allocations.

be dependent on in retirement, I want closer to a sure thing ... not a maybe.

A Half-Empty Glass — Understand clearly, mine is a cautionary brand of pessimism. You'll have to forgive me, being a millennial has certainly shaped my perspective. The American dream of going to college, getting married and buying a home to start a family has morphed, for many, into a one-way ticket to soul-crushing debt.

Millennials have witnessed nearly 20 years of a soft jobs market as opposed to a booming economy. While my father enjoyed starting his investment portfolio during the roaring 80s and 90s, stocks have taken my generation on a gut-wrenching rollercoaster.

Millennials are more cynical as a result. We don't trust what we're told; we want things explained. Show us the evidence, not the spin! The evidence tells us that while a balanced portfolio *might* be able to sustain income for life, it might also detonate prematurely. I promise you, this isn't spin; it's measurable and undeniable risk. Skeptical? I'll show you!

Right Place, Wrong Time — Sequence of Returns Risk

Mark Twain popularized the quip, "there are three kinds of lies: lies, damned lies and statistics." The financial industry abuses statistics all the time to color its marketing razzle-dazzle, push its narrative and convince you to take risks. Consider one of the more common deceptions: average rate of return.

> **Loss stinks:** Suppose you've just invested in a new mutual fund. In its first year, the fund flops, dropping 50 percent. But you don't panic and decide to ride things out. The next year the fund comes back with a vengeance and banks a 50 percent positive return. What a wild ride!
>
> When this fund launches its marketing campaign the following year, it gets to tell the investing public that the average rate of return for the previous two years is 0 percent [(-50%+50%)÷2]. New investors

wouldn't normally be thrilled with a zero, but they might be impressed that the fund was able to navigate such a volatile period while protecting investor principal. Unfortunately, the truth is far less impressive.

Suppose you originally invested $100,000. At the end of the first year, your investment would have dropped to $50,000 ($100,000 −50%). The fund rebounded the following year, bouncing back 50%, but your year-end balance is just $75,000. The fund is telling the public that it stayed even over the past 2 years when its investors lost money. Your real return is −25%. The takeaway? **Losses hurt far more than gains can help.**

Averages don't matter, but real returns do. It's not *what* you get for a return that matters but *when*. **The *order* in which you experience returns is probably the single greatest determinant of retirement success from risk-oriented assets.** If you only learn a few things from this book make this lesson one of your takeaways. Understanding sequence-of-return risk is a game changer.

I'm not suggesting it's impossible for a diversified portfolio to provide lifetime income. But understand it's quite possible for a diversified portfolio to *fail* in that same endeavor. And if your plan fails, it may have fallen victim to sequence of returns risk.

Let's explore using another example: the Starks and the Lannisters are two married couples, they each have million-dollar nest eggs and everyone is age 65. They have identical portfolios deployed 60 percent in stocks and 40 percent in bonds[44]. They both plan to withdraw $40,000 per year (following the 4% rule) to cover retirement expenses and will increase those withdrawals by 3 percent each year to offset inflation. The only difference between our two couples is going to be *when* they retire.

---

[44] The illustration uses historical annual performance data on the S&P 500 to represent stocks and the Bloomberg Barclays Capital U.S. Aggregate Bond Index to represent bonds.

The Starks retire in 1997. I've assumed our investors pay an average mutual fund expense charge of 0.50 percent and their financial advisor another 1 percent each year to manage their accounts.

Here's how the Starks make out. It's pretty good! The Starks made it to age 85 with more than 80 percent of their nest egg intact. They still have some fuel in the tank to take on their 90s, pay out-of-pocket for any extraordinary health expenses and maybe leave a sizeable inheritance for the kids.

Stark Portfolio Performance				
Year	Starting Balance	Income Withdrawal	Annual Return	Ending Balance
1997	$1,000,000	$40,000	20.97%	$1,161,274
1998	$1,161,274	$41,200	17.98%	$1,321,440
1999	$1,321,440	$42,436	9.89%	$1,405,498
2000	$1,405,498	$43,709	-2.93%	$1,321,861
2001	$1,321,861	$45,020	-5.95%	$1,200,843
2002	$1,200,843	$46,371	-11.42%	$1,022,655
2003	$1,022,655	$47,762	15.97%	$1,130,563
2004	$1,130,563	$49,195	5.63%	$1,142,250
2005	$1,142,250	$50,671	1.27%	$1,105,464
2006	$1,105,464	$52,191	8.40%	$1,141,790
2007	$1,141,790	$53,757	3.41%	$1,125,091
2008	$1,125,091	$55,369	-22.50%	$829,056
2009	$829,056	$57,030	14.94%	$887,382
2010	$887,382	$58,741	8.78%	$901,428
2011	$901,428	$60,504	1.64%	$854,682
2012	$854,682	$62,319	8.23%	$857,607
2013	$857,607	$64,188	15.45%	$916,017
2014	$916,017	$66,114	7.72%	$915,533
2015	$915,533	$68,097	-1.72%	$832,877
2016	$832,877	$70,140	5.28%	**$803,039**

Now let's check in on the Lannisters. They're retirement plan is identical with one key exception: they reached age 65 in the year 2000, right at the peak of the tech bubble. How would that have changed retiring just three years after the Starks?

	Lannister Portfolio Performance			
Year	Starting Balance	Income Withdrawal	Annual Return	Ending Balance
2000	$1,000,000	$40,000	-2.93%	$931,853
2001	$931,853	$41,200	-5.95%	$837,641
2002	$837,641	$42,436	-11.42%	$704,409
2003	$704,409	$43,709	15.97%	$766,200
2004	$766,200	$45,020	5.63%	$761,782
2005	$761,782	$46,371	1.27%	$724,511
2006	$724,511	$47,762	8.40%	$733,623
2007	$733,623	$49,195	3.41%	$707,740
2008	$707,740	$50,671	-22.50%	$509,242
2009	$509,242	$52,191	14.94%	$525,343
2010	$525,343	$53,757	8.78%	$513,011
2011	$513,011	$55,369	1.64%	$465,128
2012	$465,128	$57,030	8.23%	$441,701
2013	$441,701	$58,741	15.45%	$442,134
2014	$442,134	$60,504	7.72%	$411,100
2015	$411,100	$62,319	-1.72%	$342,789
2016	$342,789	$64,188	5.28%	$293,322
(1997)	$293,322	$66,114	20.97%	$274,845
(1998)	$274,845	$68,097	17.98%	$243,917
(1999)	$243,917	$70,140	9.89%	$190,963

To keep our comparison apples-to-apples, I used returns from 1997 to 1999 to end the Lannisters run and get them to age 85. As a result, both the Starks and the Lannisters have experienced the **exact same average rate of return** on their portfolios, but the Lannisters end up with more than **75% less**! How can this be?

This is the awful consequence of sequence of returns risk, when you're on the wrong side of it. It doesn't matter solely what your portfolio averages, but rather in what *order* it experiences good and bad years. In short, a negative run at the beginning of your retirement can have dramatic effects. The Lannisters are now just a few years away from running out of money, with no reserves for medical emergencies and little chance of leaving an inheritance. All because the market didn't cooperate with their desired timeframe.

Some of you might be puzzled. You've seen the market go down before, but it's always come back. Why hasn't sequence of returns risk stymied you? The key here is the *withdrawals*.

> **Crash course**: Imagine being ready to retire. The year is 2008. Britney Spears is the most famous woman on the planet, Brad Pitt and Angelina Jolie are still married and Senators John McCain and Barack Obama are set to square off on the presidential campaign trail. Life is good and everything seems to be rolling according to your plan.
>
> Unexpectedly, the market crashes and stocks plummet 50 percent during the worst of the decline. Seasoned employees within 10 years of retirement, like yourself, lose an average of 25 percent of their 401(k) portfolios.[45]
>
> In a panic, you contact your advisor. Are you still able to retire and get that gold watch?

---

[45] Employee Benefit Research Institute. February 2009. "The Impact of the Recent Financial Crisis on 401(k) Account Balances." https://www.ebri.org/publications/ib/?fa=ibDisp&content_id=4192.

He responds that the crash is unfortunately going to thwart your carefully laid plan. You'll need to keep working to get that money back. But don't blame him, nobody saw it coming! He advises patience, that it should only take two to five years to recover.

Now you're furious. You explain that you're tired of your boss, your back aches and you can't possibly sit in traffic another two to five years. Anxiously, you ask what the consequence would be if you were to insist on retiring despite the setback to your portfolio.

You're told this is possible, but not without consequence. If you insist on retiring, depending on your age and situation, you'll need to reduce anticipated monthly income by about 10-30% permanently. There go all the vacations.

Such is the nature of sequence of returns risk, if it doesn't work in your favor. Losing the money that took a lifetime to accumulate during the critical years in or around retirement can be devastating.

When the market has crashed during your income-producing years, your patience is rewarded when the market bounces back. But when you're retired you can't afford to be patient. You _need_ that money. And taking withdrawals into a declining market, in some cases, can make recovery a mathematical impossibility.

You might wonder why you've never heard of this risk. Well think about it. Why would money managers, who make their living by keeping you invested, want to advertise that their products and services might not be able to provide you with the lifetime income you need at the precise moment you need it most? Some of the more scrupulous advisors are frank about the risks inherent in using their services; but many aren't, or are just not well-versed in any alternatives.

T. Rowe Price released a report in 2011 titled *Dismal Decade Offers Cautionary Lessons for Retirees.*[46] They estimated that investors who retired in the year 2000, using age-appropriate blended portfolios and following the 4 percent rule for withdrawals had a 29 percent chance of running out of money in the absence of taking corrective measures to offset the bad string of market returns.

The methods suggested to get retirement back on track are all unpleasant to some degree: return to work, reduce withdrawals or discontinue inflation adjustments. All these alternatives can translate into a diminished lifestyle. Their research concluded that "retirees who take a 'set it and forget it' approach to their retirement income strategy do so at their own peril."

Morningstar contributors looked at the dilemma from a different angle in their 2013 report, *Low Bond Yields and Safe Portfolio Withdrawal Rates.*[47] While a volatile stock market is part of the problem, so too is the low bond yield environment. After all, most retirees build portfolios filled with both stocks and bonds. Recent record low interest rates have translated into subpar bond performance that fails to offset stock market volatility.

Morningstar concluded that a 4 percent withdrawal rate has, at best, a 50 percent chance of success in today's low-yield environment. They further concluded that it would be necessary to reduce retirement nest egg withdrawals to between 2-3 percent to increase the rate of success beyond 90 percent.

In other words, markets are asking retirees to take more risk and spend less money. How generous!

---

[46] T. Rowe Price. 2011. "Dismal Decade Offers Cautionary Lessons for Retirees." https://www4.troweprice.com/iws/wps/wcm/connect/e3c2ec8045961707ba69bf32e4e97423/DismalDecade.pdf?MOD=AJPERES.

[47] David Blanchett. Michael Finke. Wade D. Pfau. Morningstar. Jan. 21, 2013. "Low Bond Yields and Safe Portfolio Withdrawal Rates." https://corporate.morningstar.com/US/documents/targetmaturity/LowBondYieldsWithdrawalRates.pdf.

> **Final destination**: Imagine boarding a flight to your dream vacation destination. You've settled in, stowed your luggage and buckled your lap belt. You're about to dig into the new paperback you picked up at the newsstand when the captain comes over the intercom, "good afternoon ladies and gentlemen. Welcome aboard the aircraft. We're scheduled to reach our destination early this evening and will do our best to keep you comfortable. The crew will come around with refreshments and allow access to in-flight entertainment once we reach cruising altitude. We know you have your choice of airlines and thank you for choosing Retirement Airways. Oh, by the way, control is only giving us a 50 percent chance of making it to our destination. Try to sit back, relax and enjoy the flight."
>
> What?! Would you ever stay on that flight? Would you have even booked it in the first place? Each year we spend hours planning our vacations, but spend little time planning for retirement, which can be a 20- or 30-year vacation!

It doesn't matter if you're optimistic or pessimistic about our country's economic future. If the market doesn't cooperate during the early years of your retirement you may have problems from the start. And there's no way we can tell in advance what the market will be doing when you retire. It's a guess.

Prudence dictates that we protect some of the nest egg to help defend against this uncertainty. There's a reason the financial toolbox is vast and diverse. The markets should play a role in your retirement plan, but to depend on them entirely is done at your own peril. Injecting a level of certainty into the mix is going to require a different set of tools.

Show Me the Income

Lifetime income is the best tool for addressing our greatest retirement risk—longevity. Since many of us will make it to advanced age with relative ease, it requires that our retirement plan be up to the task of delivering income that can last as long as we do. And there are only three sources of guaranteed lifetime income available today: Social Security, pensions and annuities.

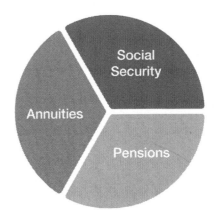

Social Security is something you'll automatically get based on a qualified work history. And either your employer will provide you with a pension or they won't; it's not something you control. That leaves annuities as the last bastion for providing guaranteed lifetime income.

Like any other financial tool, annuities have their own unique strengths and weaknesses, and they are not the right tool for everyone. But their primary purpose is to protect principal, provide guaranteed income for life or both. In an earlier chapter, we covered various annuity options available in the toolbox. You'll need to carefully consider if they make sense for you, and if so, which one might be right for your situation.

Annuities in Action

We saw earlier how sequence of returns risk can thwart even the most carefully laid plans. Let's assume we use a fixed indexed annuity to help us reduce this risk since they're able to protect principal on a contractual basis. I'm going to keep this simple and use a hypothetical fixed indexed annuity that credits interest based on the annual performance of the S&P 500. The insurance company will

credit us up to 50 percent of what the market does during a good year (calculated on your annuity anniversary) and protect our account in its entirety in a bad year. In other words, the worst thing that can happen is that we might earn 0 percent interest after a market crash. Straightforward, right?

Let's return to our friends the Starks and the Lannisters. We saw that an age-appropriate blend of stocks and bonds only worked for the Starks since the market cooperated with their retirement plans. But the poor Lannisters were on track to run out of money simply because the market crashed at the wrong time. How would circumstances have changed if our retiree friends had instead used a fixed indexed annuity to satisfy a portion of their basic income needs?

As you will see on the following page, amazingly, the Starks have not only perfectly preserved their nest egg, but modestly grown it over the 20-year stretch. In fact, the result is a 52 percent *increase* when compared with the original strategy of using a stock and bond mix to support their retirement income needs! This goes to show the potential power of avoiding market losses in retirement.

But the real question is whether this same strategy would improve the fate of the Lannisters. We know they're about to retire into the thick of a market maelstrom. Let's see what the fixed indexed annuity accomplishes for their situation.

Stark Annuity Solution				
Year	Starting Balance	Income W/D	S&P 500	Annuity ROR	Ending Balance
1997	$1,000,000	$40,000	31.01%	15.51%	$1,108,848
1998	$1,108,848	$41,200	26.67%	13.34%	$1,210,019
1999	$1,210,019	$42,436	19.53%	9.77%	$1,281,597
2000	$1,281,597	$43,709	-10.14%	0.00%	$1,237,888
2001	$1,237,888	$45,020	-13.04%	0.00%	$1,192,868
2002	$1,192,868	$46,371	-23.37%	0.00%	$1,146,497
2003	$1,146,497	$47,762	26.38%	13.19%	$1,243,658
2004	$1,243,658	$49,195	8.99%	4.50%	$1,248,154
2005	$1,248,154	$50,671	3.00%	1.50%	$1,215,446
2006	$1,215,446	$52,191	13.62%	6.81%	$1,242,472
2007	$1,242,472	$53,757	3.53%	1.77%	$1,209,696
2008	$1,209,696	$55,369	-38.49%	0.00%	$1,154,327
2009	$1,154,327	$57,030	23.45%	11.73%	$1,225,955
2010	$1,225,955	$58,741	12.78%	6.39%	$1,241,798
2011	$1,241,798	$60,504	0.00%	0.00%	$1,181,295
2012	$1,181,295	$62,319	13.41%	6.71%	$1,194,003
2013	$1,194,003	$64,188	29.60%	14.80%	$1,297,028
2014	$1,297,028	$66,114	11.39%	5.70%	$1,301,014
2015	$1,301,014	$68,097	-0.73%	0.00%	$1,232,917
2016	$1,232,917	$70,140	9.54%	4.77%	**$1,218,241**

Year	Starting Balance	Income W/D	S&P 500	Annuity ROR	Ending Balance
Lannister Annuity Solution					
2000	$1,000,000	$40,000	-10.14%	0.00%	$960,000
2001	$960,000	$41,200	-13.04%	0.00%	$918,800
2002	$918,800	$42,436	-23.37%	0.00%	$876,364
2003	$876,364	$43,709	26.38%	13.19%	$942,482
2004	$942,482	$45,020	8.99%	4.50%	$937,803
2005	$937,803	$46,371	3.00%	1.50%	$904,803
2006	$904,803	$47,762	13.62%	6.81%	$915,406
2007	$915,406	$49,195	3.53%	1.77%	$881,499
2008	$881,499	$50,671	-38.49%	0.00%	$830,828
2009	$830,828	$52,191	23.45%	11.73%	$869,933
2010	$869,933	$53,757	12.78%	6.39%	$868,330
2011	$868,330	$55,369	0.00%	0.00%	$812,960
2012	$812,960	$57,030	13.41%	6.71%	$806,615
2013	$806,615	$58,741	29.60%	14.80%	$858,559
2014	$858,559	$60,504	11.39%	5.70%	$843,505
2015	$843,505	$62,319	-0.73%	0.00%	$781,186
2016	$781,186	$64,188	9.54%	4.77%	$751,199
(1997)	$751,199	$66,114	31.01%	15.51%	$791,307
(1998)	$791,307	$68,097	26.67%	13.34%	$819,650
(1999)	$819,650	$70,140	19.53%	9.77%	**$822,699**

What a difference! Sequence of returns risk had ravaged their retirement in the first scenario when they depended on their portfolio of stocks and bonds to provide lifetime income. But even without any luck on their side, suffering three consecutive years of stagnation at the earliest stages of retirement, the fixed indexed annuity protected the integrity of their income plan. They're able to stay on course, take anticipated withdrawals to meet their retirement income needs and have plenty of fuel left for the years to come.

A few things to note—obviously, these examples reflect past performance only, and can't be used to predict how the markets will perform in the future. The withdrawals, as is true with most investment disbursements, may be subject to taxation. And lastly, all annuity guarantees are backed by the financial strength and claims-paying ability of the issuing company—which means that the guarantees are only as strong as the company backing them.

Rails of Steel — Income is the Key

When you're retired, it means the paychecks have stopped coming in. The objective is to create your own income, to have a plan that can provide lifetime income with as little risk of interruption or failure as possible. Social Security and pensions may get you part of the way, but the rest is up to your nest egg. And while the stock market *might* provide a steady source of income it might also implode, possibly without a strong chance of recovery.

Annuities can be a great solution for reducing volatility and can be the right solution when additional GAP-fighting income is necessary. In many cases, it's only necessary to protect a portion of the nest egg with an annuity to satisfy your income goal. This is ideal; remember that annuities have restrictions on liquidity so we'll want to put your remaining assets to work elsewhere.

But we'll return to the world of investing a little later. Now that we know how to lay a strong foundation for retirement income,

let's turn our focus to another risk that can seriously derail our plans: contending with an unplanned health care event.

ON-TRACK INCOME FOCUS

Have you identified how to maximize your guaranteed sources of retirement income? Have you measured the potential impact of a market crash? Are you confident in your nest egg's ability to provide income that can last a lifetime?

Call us today to review your lifetime income strategy (888) AR-CADIA, or visit us online at www.railsofsteel.com.

CHAPTER SIX

Health Care

"If you can't afford a doctor, go to an airport... you'll get a free X ray and breast exam... and if you mention al Qaeda, you'll get a free colonoscopy!"

—*Internet meme*

An unexpected health event can unravel the best-laid plans for retirement. I believe that we're amid a full-blown medical crisis in this country, where quality of care, availability and costs are moving in the wrong direction. Major differences will be felt between those who plan for the unexpected and those who simply hope for the best.

We truly cannot afford to dismiss this risk. A recent study by Fidelity Investments estimates that the average couple will experience $260,000 in out-of-pocket costs for health care during their retirement! [41]

This chapter is designed to walk you through the transition from preretirement medical insurance to Medicare and what happens beyond. We'll cover features, benefits, advantages and risks associated with Medicare, supplemental plans, Medicaid and long-term care insurance. Buckle up, there's a lot to cover. Don't say I didn't warn you!

Medicare

At age 65 most Americans become eligible for Medicare, a federal single-payer insurance program that is administered through a network of private insurance companies. It's been the mainstay for retiree medical coverage since Congress enacted it in 1965 under Title XVIII of the Social Security Act.

To be eligible for Medicare, you or your spouse must have been employed and paid FICA tax for 40 quarters. These quarters do not need to be continuous or consecutive. If this milestone is achieved, Medicare Part A is "free"—though you did pay for this benefit via taxes deducted from your pay while working. Those that cannot satisfy the FICA requirement can still purchase Medicare Part A, but it's no bargain—you'll pay up to $413 per month in 2017.

Our discussion of Medicare will its four core plans:

Part A — Hospital insurance

Part B — Physician and outpatient care

Part C — Medicare Advantage plans

Part D — Prescription drug plans

At enrollment, you'll have a choice: sign up for the combination of Parts A and B, known as Original Medicare or choose Part C—a Medicare Advantage plan. There are pros and cons with each:

Original Medicare, which combines hospital and physician coverages, forms the foundation of the health insurance to which most Americans are accustomed. It allows you to choose your own doctor or care facilities provided they accept Medicare reimbursement for services. But any expenses not covered by Medicare are your responsibility. Those coverage gaps typically require some sort of supplemental insurance.

Medicare Advantage (MA) plans vary by state and availability but function similarly to a health marketing organization (HMO) network. In-network, basic medical services are reimbursed by Medicare, as are certain ancillary costs that would typically be covered with a supplemental plan. The tradeoff is that MA plans limit your care to an approved network of health care facilities, doctors and other medical professionals.

Let's break it down: with Original Medicare, your care provider options are effectively unlimited but there are more out-of-pocket costs. Meanwhile, MA plans are less costly but fewer care provider options are available within the select network. Choosing between Original Medicare and an MA plan should be considered carefully based on your needs and the plans available in your area.

Medicare Option Comparison		
	Provider Options	**Ancillary Costs**
Original Medicare	Many	Your responsibility
Medicare Advantage (MA)	Fewer	Covered

Part D prescription drug coverage must be purchased separately for Original Medicare participants but is usually, but not always, included in MA plans.

Enrollment in Medicare is easy, but the mechanics vary depending on the route chosen. Since Medicare is tied to Social Security, those who collect their retirement benefits prior to age 65 are automatically enrolled in Parts A and B. The Centers for Medicare &

Medicaid Services, the federal agency that administers Medicare, will mail you a Medicare card three months prior to your 65th birthday.

For those planning to begin collecting Social Security beyond age 65, enrolling in Medicare does *not* require that you collect Social Security benefits.

Timely enrollment is encouraged, as penalties may apply for enrollment beyond age 65. Tardiness also risks a gap in your coverage. The switch to Medicare should be started well in advance, especially for those transitioning from employer-sponsored plans. Those wanting a MA plan must simply select their plan prior to their 65th birthday.

Individuals or families that will have health insurance beyond age 65 through an employer or alternate source can delay enrollment in Medicare Parts B and D without penalty. When this alternative health insurance ends, to remain compliant and avoid penalties, Part B insurance must be purchased no more than eight months following retirement and Part D within 63 days of retirement. Due to the complexity of Medicare rules and timelines, it is highly recommended that you consult with your financial advisor and employer at least six months before your 65th birthday.

What's This Going to Cost Me? — While Medicare Part A hospital coverage costs nothing for most enrollees, the average Part B premium for physician and outpatient services is $109 per month in 2017. Part B coverage is optional. However, you'll most likely want to have it unless you have comprehensive coverage through another source.

Medicare Part B covers services and supplies that are medically necessary to treat your health conditions that can include outpatient care, preventive services (such as flu shots and physical exams), ambulance services and durable medical equipment. It also covers part-time or intermittent home health and rehabilitation services.

MA plan participants will pay their Part B premium in addition to the cost of the MA plan, which can range from $0 to several hundred dollars per month. With most MA plans, additional out-of-pocket expenses such as copayments, deductibles and coinsurance are capped annually at $6,700 in 2017.

In 2017, Original Medicare participants are responsible for the following deductibles:

Part A — Covers basic inpatient hospital stays. In addition, skilled nursing, home health and hospice care are covered. Most participants will pay no premium, but it will be your responsibility to pay a $1,316 deductible for hospital stays.

Part B — Covers doctor visits, preventive care and most outpatient services. A $183 annual deductible for this coverage applies.

Part D — Is the prescription drug plan. It varies in cost depending on the options available in your area, but currently averages $34 per month.

Most Part D plans have a coverage gap nicknamed the "donut hole." This gap is triggered when the cost of covered prescriptions reaches $3,700 in 2017. Beyond this point you'll pay up to 40 percent of the cost of covered brand name drugs and 51 percent of the cost of generic drugs.

Medigap (Supplemental Insurance) — The out-of-pocket expenses associated with Original Medicare can quickly become burdensome for some participants, especially those with chronic or serious conditions. Medigap is additional insurance you can buy from a private company to pay health care expenses not covered by Original Medicare such as copays and deductibles. Medigap policies purchased after 2006 *do not* cover prescription costs.

There are 10 standard Medigap policies lettered A through N, which vary in both cost and benefits provided. Plans range from as little as $50 to several hundred dollars per month. Choosing the right plan depends entirely upon your needs, so consider your options carefully. The following table compares Medigap plans based on some, but certainly not all, attributes.

Benefits	MediGap[48] Plans									
	A	B	C	D	F*	G	K	L	M	N
Part A coinsurance and hospital costs (up to 365 days after Medicare benefits are used up)	Y	Y	Y	Y	Y	Y	Y	Y	Y	Y
Part B coinsurance or copayment	Y	Y	Y	Y	Y	Y	50%	75%	Y	Y***
Blood (first 3 pints)	Y	Y	Y	Y	Y	Y	50%	75%	Y	Y
Part A hospice care coinsurance or copayment	Y	Y	Y	Y	Y	Y	50%	75%	Y	Y
Skilled nursing facility care coinsurance	N	N	Y	Y	Y	Y	50%	75%	Y	Y
Part A deductible	N	Y	Y	Y	Y	Y	50%	75%	50%	Y
Part B deductible	N	N	Y	N	Y	N	N	N	N	N
Part B excess charge	N	N	N	N	Y	Y	N	N	N	N
Foreign travel exchange (up to plan limits)	N	N	80%	80%	80%	80%	N	N	80%	80%
Out-of-pocket limit**							$5,120	$2,560		

[48] Medicare.gov. 2017. "How to Compare Medigap Policies." https://www.medicare.gov/supplement-other-insurance/compare-medigap/compare-medigap.html.

* Plan F also offers a high-deductible plan. If you choose this option, this means you must pay for Medicare-covered costs up to the deductible amount of $2,200 in 2017 before your Medigap plan pays anything.

** After you meet your out-of-pocket yearly limit and your yearly Part B deductible, the Medigap plan pays 100 percent of covered services for the rest of the calendar year.

*** Plan N pays 100 percent of the Part B coinsurance, except for a copayment of up to $20 for some office visits and up to a $50 copayment for emergency room visits that don't result in inpatient admission.

Deer in the Headlights — You may be feeling confused, overwhelmed or perhaps a little angry. I felt the same way just *writing* much of this chapter! Medicare is needlessly dense and hopelessly bureaucratic. What a stress-inducing nightmare. But it's the system we've got, so we have to make peace with it. On the bright side, 75 percent of Medicare recipients appear to enjoy their Medicare coverage and believe it to be working well. [49]

Care needs and cost sensitivities are highly individualized, so what you do from here is largely up to you. Most Americans are enrolled in Original Medicare, the total annual cost of which is $3,215 in 2017 (assumes you sign up for Parts A, B and D with all premiums and deductibles included). This estimate does not include Part A coinsurance or the premiums associated with the Medigap coverage you may elect.

It's worth noting that Medicare does not cover the following expenses, so plan accordingly:

- Alternative medicine
- Cosmetic surgery
- Routine dental care (checkups, cleanings, fillings, dentures)
- Vision care (exams, refractions, lenses and glasses),

---

[49] Dan Mangan. CNBC. July 17, 2015. "Medicare, Medicaid Popularity High: Kaiser". https://www.cnbc.com/2015/07/16/medicare-medicaid-popularity-high-ahead-of-birthday.html.

- Foot care (podiatry)
- Hearing exams or hearing aids
- Services performed outside of the United States

Long-Term Care (LTC)

Medicare covers what it characterizes as medically necessary and routine care: doctor visits, prescription drugs, emergencies, hospital stays, etc.

Medicare will also provide coverage for short-term services for conditions that are expected to *improve*. Events such as physical therapy following a fall or a stroke, short-term skilled nursing care, social services and certain medical supplies are covered if they are deemed medically necessary and your doctor re-orders them every 60 days.

However, Medicare provides only scant coverage for the most expensive medical exposures: long-term care. **An LTC event can be defined as any contiguous outpatient event that lasts longer than 100 days. Medicare will typically cover costs for the initial 100-day period, but beyond that, you're on your own.**

A Freudian Slip-up — Famed psychoanalyst Sigmund Freud once claimed that people tend not to fear death because they struggle to believe in the possibility of their own demise. He believed the unconscious mind ignores the passage of time and mortality, resulting in our being irrational concerning these same issues.

How we interpret mortality is both personal and highly emotional. But on a societal level, Freud's observation helps to explain the widespread avoidance of one of the most important elements of retirement planning — the need for long-term care.

According to a study by the Associated Press, two-thirds of Americans age 40 and older have done little or no planning for LTC. The most common reason? An erroneous belief that Medicare covers it.[50]

This reluctance to address serious, long-term medical needs is easy to understand. Discussion of being dependent on others is profoundly unpleasant. Few things can be as emotionally charged or crushingly expensive as a long-term care event. Unfortunately, choosing to ignore this risk or pushing it to the fringes can have devastating effects on you, your family and even your community.

Courage Through Action — During the next 30 years, Americans will require more long-term care than ever before. The quality of care you receive, the extent to which your family may be burdened and the overall cost deserves serious consideration.

Developmental psychologist Erik Erikson observed that people eventually come to terms with mortality, but only as we age or witness the passing of close relatives or friends. Unfortunately, by the time we come to terms with these issues, it can be long after it's possible to plan for them financially.

Creating a financial plan with an eye on end of life scenarios takes mental courage, requiring consideration of things that are decidedly unpleasant or that may seem impossible for us to experience. But to conquer these notions and to plan prudently despite them, is key to developing a plan as strong as steel—one that works through both sickness and health.

Just the Facts — An LTC event is commonly defined as a point in time when a person requires assistance with basic, everyday functions known as activities of daily living (ADLs). There are six

---

[50] Emily Swanson. The Associated Press. U.S. News and World Report. May 25, 2017. "Poll: Older Americans Want Medicare-Covered Long-Term Care." https://www.us-news.com/news/business/articles/2017-05-25/older-americans-want-medicare-to-pay-for-long-term-care.

basic ADLs: eating, bathing, dressing, toileting, transferring (walking) and continence.

Many people falsely assume that needing assistance with ADLs is a result exclusive to Alzheimer's or dementia. Yet, a host of medical problems can trigger the need for ADL assistance, some of the more common being mobility issues and cancer. Other common LTC issues include: arthritis, congestive heart disease, head injuries, pneumonia, vision and hearing limitations. Many consider LTC to be a last resort, something to be avoided at all costs. But many people incurring an LTC event live comfortable and fulfilling lives. They simply require assistance along the way.

According to the U.S. Department of Health and Human Services, 70 percent of people age 65 and older can expect to require some form of LTC during their lives.[51] That's a staggeringly high probability! People approaching retirement sometimes struggle with this statistic, especially if they have not personally observed a close friend, neighbor or family member using home or facilitative care.

The great news is that 80 percent of people receiving LTC assistance are doing so in private homes or in the community; only 20 percent require full-time facilitative care.[52] That's a big silver lining; most people understandably fear being dependent on others. Unfortunately, even the temporary or intermittent help we're statistically likely to need is very expensive.

---

[51] LongTermCare.gov. 2017. "Who Needs Care?" https://longtermcare.acl.gov/the-basics/who-needs-care.html.

[52] Congressional Budget Office. June 26, 2013. "Rising Demand for Long-Term Services and Supports for Elderly People." https://www.cbo.gov/publication/44363.

The Cost of LTC — While costs for LTC vary greatly from state to state, the national average for home health care and assisted living is about $4,000 per month. A private room in a full-time care facility is nearly double that, around $8,000 per month.[53]

We know the costs, but the bigger question is how much you might need to *spend*. This is entirely dependent on the duration of your care event. The average person needing LTC services will require three years of care. However, there's a noteworthy disparity between the experience of men and women. On average, men require 2.2 years of care while women require 3.7 years. The difference is due to women having longer life expectancies and thus having a greater likelihood of not only requiring care, but also receiving services for longer periods of time.

So, what can you expect to pay for long-term care? Let's crunch some numbers. The following table demonstrates possible outcomes for a married couple assuming a three-year average for care events:

Considering Long-Term Care Costs for Two				
			If She Needs...	
		No Care	Home or Assisted Care	Facilitative Care
And He Needs...	No Care	$0	$144,000	$288,000
	Home or Assisted Care	$144,000	$288,000	$432,000
	Facilitative Care	$288,000	$432,000	$576,000

[53] Genworth Financial. 2017. "Genworth 2017 Cost of Care Survey." https://www.genworth.com/about-us/industry-expertise/cost-of-care.html.

These costs are astronomical—talk about sticker shock! What can you do about it?

Nothing — Many American simply ignore the issue altogether; it's too uncomfortable to consider dependency in our golden years. Others assume that these problems won't affect them or if they do, they'll be too infirm or "out-of-it" to care. Many more think the expense is too high to address seriously, so they roll the dice and hope for the best.

This thinking is dangerously naive. Given the probabilities and the cost, the only prudent thing to do is to plan as effectively as possible with the resources available. There's more riding on it than dollars and cents.

First, there's quality of care to consider. There will inevitably be wide disparity in the care experience between people who have financially prepared versus those who will depend on government assistance. According to the Association of American Medical Colleges, the per-capita number of physicians, particularly in specialties catering to seniors, is shrinking at a time when the growth of the senior population is booming. In other words, demand is increasing while the supply is dwindling! This could potentially lead to longer wait times for appointments, a decline in the quality of care and greater risk for urgent health issues.

The second consideration that often falls to the wayside is who pays the price when there's no plan for LTC. In my experience, in the absence of a plan, children, siblings, friends and neighbors sacrifice time, career opportunities and personal expense to assist loved ones. It's one thing to be dependent on others, but entirely something else to be a burden to the people we care about most.

Failure to plan might even be viewed as selfish given the demands it can impose on others. There are few things we love more than our children and extended family; one of the best ways to show it is to thoughtfully plan for our own LTC needs. While it's certainly easy to ignore the likelihood of needing LTC, we owe it to ourselves and our family to do better.

Medicaid — Not to be confused with Medicare, *Medicaid* is a state-managed program that can cover many LTC expenses. But eligibility is difficult and may require advanced planning.

Medicaid is a welfare benefit designed to backstop people who run out of financial options. In most states, you must reduce your assets to less than $2,000 to qualify. Some assets are protected, such as your primary residence, personal property, home furnishings, one motor vehicle, a limited amount of spousal assets and assets held in special kinds of trusts, which we'll discuss later.

For most readers, Medicaid is an option of last resort and best avoided, if possible. Because even if financial qualifications are met your care will be subject to the whims of a state bureaucracy, not to mention the uncertain vagaries of political trends.

Estate-Planning Maneuvers — Can you legally "hide" your money and assets in a trust and effectively prevent them from thwarting Medicaid eligibility? Yes. Is there a catch? You bet!

Clients frequently ask if a trust can place their money beyond the reach of the "system" and help them become eligible for Medicaid. Besides the seldom-considered ethical quandary of hiding your own money so your neighbors (taxpayers) can foot the bill instead, let's cover what makes this maneuvering so tricky to execute.

Revocable Trusts

As we'll discuss later in our chapter on estate planning, revocable trusts can be great tools for probate avoidance and creating a legacy. But Medicaid considers all assets inside a revocable trust to be fair game; these trusts do nothing to protect your assets from the cost of medical care.

Irrevocable Trusts

If you're going to get serious about sheltering assets from the medical system, you're going to need an irrevocable trust. But the trust must be established in such a way that the grantor, be it a single person or a married couple, has no access to or ability to distribute any assets to themselves. In other words, if you can touch the money, Medicaid will force you to use it before helping you out.

You will also be required to satisfy a *five-year look-back*. Any assets transferred to the irrevocable trust within five years of the medical event will be ineligible from protection and subject to penalty. This means irrevocable trusts need to be funded well in advance. Last-minute shuffling won't cut it.

There's one useful caveat. If you set up an irrevocable trust to distribute income, but functionally cut off all other access, only the income will be counted against your Medicaid eligibility.

Irrevocable trusts offer medical protection because you are giving up control and access to the assets within. It's almost like providing your intended beneficiaries their inheritance while you're still alive. It can make great sense for people of considerable means who may want to shelter some, but not all their wealth. But many people struggle with the thought of losing control of their money.

> **Clever maneuvering:** Suppose a married couple in their 80s discovers that the husband is facing a medical event that will require 24-hour skilled nursing care. The wife's priority is to get her husband the best care possible, but she's anxious that the associated costs will tear through their savings, possibly leaving her destitute.
>
> They might work with an advisor and estate planning attorney to place most of their assets in an irrevocable trust, leaving enough outside of it to cover the anticipated costs of the husband's care for the next five years. The assets placed in trust will not have any protection until the five-year look-back is satisfied. But if he still needs care beyond that time, the trust would be fully seasoned, protecting the rest of the money and making any ongoing care eligible for Medicaid

reimbursement. The trust could be designed to provide the wife with steady income to see her through the rest of her retirement.

What did they accomplish? Notably, they retained full control over their assets until the care event began. And though they were responsible for paying the husband's care out-of-pocket for the first five years, they protected the rest of the assets. Finally, the plan provided financial security for the wife.

Certainly, the couple would have spent a lot of money on health care during those first five years; trust planning is far from perfect. But the benefits are clear. Your financial advisor can put you in touch with an estate planning attorney who can help you explore trusts and other legal steps that may be beneficial to your situation.

Gifts

Some people are under the impression that you make gifts to family to get assets out of your name and advance eligibility for Medicaid. This can be true. However, timing and amounts matter. You can gift a maximum of $14,000 per person per year without incurring tax liability. Regardless of the amount given, the transfers need to have been made at least five years prior to applying for Medicaid lest they be subject to the look-back penalty.

Look Back Penalty: All asset transfers, whether they are gifts or assets moved to trust, are subject to this look-back. Violating this rule is tricky since the penalty applied is measured in <u>time</u>. Here's how it works:

The state will take the amount gifted and divide it by the average monthly cost of care in your area. The average monthly cost is known as the penalty divisor. In Massachusetts and New Hampshire, this divisor is about $10,000 per month. The result of the calculation is the amount of time that Medicaid benefits will be withheld. For example: If you gave away $100,000 in violation of the five-year look-back, Medicaid would withhold benefits for 10 months ($100,000 ÷ $10,000 = 10).

What if that was the last $100,000 you had in the world and there was no getting it back? How would you pay for your care during the

10-month penalty period? Good question; it's one that thousands of seniors contend with every year when they run afoul of the rules. Please note that this penalty begins on the date you become Medicaid eligible, not the date on which you made the gift.

These limitations aside, gifting is a great way to reduce your taxable estate. It comes with the added benefit of watching your loved ones enjoy your money while you're still living.

Assigning Property to Children or Other Relatives

We hear too often about people transferring the deed to their property to children or other relatives to advance eligibility toward Medicaid. Please think twice before doing so, your home is already exempted from Medicaid consideration. And if the person to whom you transfer the home ever becomes bankrupt, gets sued, goes through divorce, predeceases you or the relationship sours, you could be removed from your own home. It's simply not worth the risk, in my experience.

Self-Insurance — People with substantial net worth can carve out some of their savings specifically to be set aside for LTC costs. This is known as self-insuring since the burden of paying for care sits squarely on your shoulders.

The advantage of self-insurance is that it's probably the most cost-effective way to address LTC if the risk never materializes. If you never require LTC during your lifetime, no dollars or extraordinary measures were spent addressing a risk that never occurred.

But if you do get sick, ill or injured during retirement, self-insuring can be tremendously expensive, depending on the duration of care. This can have serious consequences if a surviving spouse is left impoverished or if you intend to provide an inheritance to heirs. The decision to self-insure should not be made lightly.

If we assume that the cost of home health care and/or assisted living is about $4,000 per month and the average duration of care is about three years, then a married couple would need to set aside $288,000 today to be considered adequately self-insured. To be fully protected against the cost of full-time facilitative care, the amount put aside would need to be roughly double: $576,000. Single, divorced or widowed individuals can simply halve these numbers to calculate their self-insurance needs.

The funds should be invested to keep pace with the rising cost of care. Experts, having observed changes to the cost of LTC services over the last five years, say the absolute lowest rate of inflation you should assume is about 3 percent.[54]

Self-insuring only works if the funds are unattached to any other financial goals. In other words, if you plan on dipping into those funds to buy a car or go on vacation, you'd be violating the integrity of your plan. Self-insuring requires that those funds be "out-of-sight and out-of-mind" unless a health event is incurred. Given all these commitments, the decision to self-insure is often reserved for high net worth individuals.

LTC Insurance — LTC insurance was introduced to the U.S. marketplace in 1974 as a solution to help consumers contend with nursing home expenses not covered by Medicare.

The first several iterations of LTC insurance products were far from perfect. Many policies were confusing and paid claims in only the narrowest of circumstances. Insurers began to create more consumer-friendly products as state regulators caught up to speed in the mid-to-late 80s. The timing was perfect as baby boomers began reaching their 50s in the 1990s and LTC planning began reaching their collective radar screens.

The stars were set to align. An aging population finally had a solution to defend against a risk with 70 percent probability. LTC insurance looked highly desirable. Why bear that risk out-of-

---

[54] Genworth. 2016. "Cost of Care: Summary of 2016 Survey Findings." https://www.genworth.com/dam/Americas/US/PDFs/Consumer/corporate/131168_050516.pdf.

pocket when it could be passed to a third party in exchange for a reasonable premium?

Unfortunately, LTC insurance didn't initially fare so well. Insurers badly underpriced their policies for much of the 1990s and well into the 2000s. They significantly underestimated the frequency with which policyholders would file claims and overestimated how often policy owners would cancel or allow policies to lapse.

Insurance actuaries made bad predictions about policyholder life expectancy, average care duration and the cost of eldercare services. Underwriting standards were too loose and technological advances that extend life came too rapidly, dramatically increasing longevity and the need for LTC.

America entering a low interest rate environment certainly didn't help matters. Few guessed that interest rates would go this low for this long and few industries felt the impact as acutely as this new branch of the insurance industry. Insurance companies, by regulation, keep most of their reserves in corporate, mortgage-backed or government bonds. Low yields eroded profitability and jeopardized the ability of these reserves to meet anticipated claims. It was a perfect storm of growing pains, poor decisions and bad luck.

To remain solvent, many insurance companies appealed to state insurance commissioners to raise rates on existing polices. In some cases, policy owners were required to absorb premium increases of 40 percent to retain coverage!

The effect was two-fold: increasingly, consumers began to distrust and dislike LTC insurance. In addition, many insurance companies threw in the towel and abandoned new sales. At one time, more than 100 insurers offered LTC products. Fewer than 10 percent of those companies remain, with many reputable players having withdrawn including Prudential, Allianz, MetLife and MassMutual.

LTC Design — But this isn't to say that LTC insurance is not a viable option. In fact, the companies and products that have endured this gauntlet have emerged stronger, providing excellent, cost-effective coverage. Still, consumers who might otherwise forgive LTC insurance for its rocky past continue to give it a pass because they assume the costs are astronomical. Let's take a closer look.

Assume we want to insure against what is statistically most likely to happen — we'll need LTC in an assisted living or home care setting for three years at a cost of $4,000 per month. Let's further stipulate that we're married and want to insure both adults.

In designing an LTC policy, we'd start by making sure it can pay the $4,000 per month for six years (the combined average care duration for both adults). This would create a shared pool of benefits of $288,000 known as the *policy limit*. This is the maximum amount of insurance benefits you can collect over time.

LTC policies do not have dollar deductibles. Their equivalent is what's called an *elimination period*, the amount of time that must pass before the policy will pay benefits. A 90-day elimination period is recommended as this prevents policy benefits from overlapping with coverage already provided by Medicare.

The final consideration is *inflation protection*. Today, LTC may cost $4,000 per month, but what will it cost in 20-30 years? Inflation protection increases your benefits each year so your policy keeps pace with rising health care costs. As we discussed earlier, most industry professionals suggest that inflation protection be no less than 3 percent. At that rate, a policy capable of paying up to $288,000 today will double its protection to $576,000 in a little over 20 years, when you're more likely to file a claim.

There are other features and benefits to consider, but we can stop here. We've designed a straightforward policy capable of covering an average care experience. To recap, our policy will reimburse up to $4,000 per month for six years with a 90-day elimination period and 3 percent inflation protection. I know what you're wondering — what's it cost?

The price depends on *when* you purchase it. The policy we've designed in this section might cost the couple a total of $300 to 600 per month depending on age and health history. LTC insurance costs the least when purchased in your 50s and in good health. Premiums climb steadily with age and diminished health. Getting the protection while young and healthy can make things a lot easier on your retirement budget.

As you get older, it becomes considerably more difficult to obtain LTC protection. In my experience, around 50 percent of LTC insurance applicants are declined due to pre-existing health conditions. This may seem unfair, but insurance companies must be selective when constructing their risk pools. They're not charities and, given the high claims rate, margins are razor thin.

Underwriters anticipate that 35-50 percent of policyholders will file a claim for benefits at some point during retirement. Imagine how expensive or restrictive homeowner's insurance might be if half the houses in the neighborhood were expected to burn down in the next 30 years!

Sometimes people delay buying insurance because they want to keep the cost of insurance off the monthly budget for as long as possible. But the real concern should be to apply for coverage before your doctor finds some malady that makes you *ineligible* for protection.

When you hear of couple's insurance policies, about two-thirds of the cost would be associated with the wife's share of coverage. Insurance companies aren't being sexist. Women live longer than men and are expected to require more care. Given this information, if one spouse ends up being uninsurable, we can quickly estimate the cost of covering the other partner.

We've described an entry-level policy, the Toyota Corolla of policies if you will. What would a Cadillac policy look like? Start by doubling the policy limit to cover the full cost of facilitative care — $8,000 per month. The elimination period can stay the same, but we might want to raise inflation protection to 5 percent. Since we're effectively doubling the most critical policy elements, premiums will follow suit and roughly double. Cadillac policies are more appropriate for those with higher net worth or extraordinary health or asset protection concerns.

LTC Review — Is LTC insurance the way to go? You now have enough basic information to judge for yourself. The National Association of Insurance Commissioners recommends that retirees spend no more than 7 percent of their retirement income on LTC protection. Though LTC insurance has come a long way, there are other options to consider.

Though the odds of needing LTC protection are compellingly high, retirees are simply not purchasing LTC insurance in large numbers. It's estimated that only 25 percent of baby boomers have any kind of LTC insurance.

This has perplexed the insurance industry for decades. Why are people largely ignoring the one solution specifically designed to combat the extraordinary risks and costs of an LTC event? Perhaps these actuaries should have more closely studied their Freud.

Remember, if something is uncomfortable to consider, by and large it will be ignored. You can logically lay out the risks, statistic by statistic, and, in my experience, the average person will just shrug it off:

"Too expensive."

"I'm just going to roll the dice."

"If I ever get to that point in my life, I won't care what happens to me."

These are not rational responses. They're emotional reactions that our subconscious is throwing up to defend our fragile minds from uncomfortable thoughts. I truly believe that the cost of insurance pales in comparison to the expense, burden and stress of an actual LTC event in the absence of preparation. You need a plan that provides the best and most convenient care for you and your family.

Interestingly, the insurance industry found an alternate way to reach its target audience by introducing a solution that is less uncomfortable and more familiar, something many of us already understand and are probably already implementing: life insurance.

Life Insurance

While death is every bit as unpleasant to consider as the need for long-term care, life insurance has been part of the American fabric for well over a century. It's often provided as an employer benefit, but even individual policies are usually affordable and come with all sorts of ancillary benefits like cash values, the ability to use it as collateral on loans, etc. Nearly two-thirds of American households have life insurance protection.[55]

The insurance industry has long been analyzing the reasons people are reluctant to purchase LTC insurance. We already know most: it's linked to an unpleasant event; it's thought to be expensive; and, if unused, provides no ancillary benefit to the estate.

Along the way the insurance industry made an astute observation. When an LTC event occurs, the patient isn't typically patched up and sent back to the golf course. Most LTC events occur near the end of our lives. So, the life insurance industry asked itself an important question: would it affect profitability if policyholders were given access to benefits while living to address medical expenses, rather than hold back benefits until the insured passes away?

In short, the answer they came up with is, "no." Many insurance companies determined they could give policyholders more flexible

---

[55] Jay MacDonald. Bankrate. July 8, 2015. "Survey: How Many of Us Have Life Insurance? And How Many Have Enough of It?" http://www.bankrate.com/finance/insurance/money-pulse-0715.aspx.

access to benefits without risking reserves or profitability. Today, it's possible to purchase life insurance that grants living benefit access for qualified LTC expenses at little or no additional cost. Be sure to shop amongst reputable companies and conduct thorough due diligence on product design and limitations.

Most Americans already own life insurance. Existing policies can sometimes be leveraged or transferred to provide this highly desirable LTC protection. Life insurance is also *guaranteed* to benefit someone, whether it be the insured for medical expenses or the beneficiaries at death. The premiums are never wasted.

Life Insurance Example: Some of the better life insurance policies for addressing this issue, in my opinion, are a type of universal life insurance that leverages premiums to maximize living benefits.

The way it works can be illustrated with a hypothetical example. A $100,000 premium would provide approximately the following benefits for a 55-year-old male:[56]

- A $120,000 death benefit

- A $5,000/mo living benefit to offset LTC expenses, lasting six years with 3 percent inflation protection

- A 100 percent premium refund feature available after the fifth contract anniversary

Suppose you have idle cash in the bank earning a pittance for interest. $100,000 could instead be put to work with this life insurance policy, providing a $120,000 death benefit for your estate. Better yet, should you experience an LTC event, the policy could provide a total of $360,000 of protection over six years! The inflation protection keeps the benefits growing such that 20 years down the road the total benefit pool can expand to $720,000 or more. And just in case you

---

[56] This example is hypothetical in nature and does not represent any specific product. Your actual results will vary based on a number of factors, including your age, health, insurance company and product selected, and more.

> need the money back, you can cancel the policy and be refunded your $100,000 in full after the fifth contract anniversary.

Not everyone will have idle cash on hand to give this strategy liftoff, but some companies will let you break up the premium obligation over a 10-year period to make things easier. Sometimes other options are right under your nose. Remember, if you have any existing life insurance, policy cash values may be directed toward a new policy with LTC protection. Availability is subject to state regulation and medical underwriting.

Conclusion — How to best engage Medicare and then coordinate it with strategies to contend with LTC exposure is a vast and nuanced topic. The decisions you make will affect the quality of your health care, your retirement budget, estate plan and the protection provided to your family.

Our holistic planning process is designed to approach these issues with the care they deserve. Everyone's situation is different, so gaining a good understanding of your options, rooted in education, is the best place to start.

ON-TRACK HEALTH CARE FOCUS

Have you decided whether to enroll in Original Medicare or Medicare Advantage? Have you measured how a long-term-care event may impact your autonomy, assets and family? Have you reviewed all eligible legal, financial and insurance options for protection?

Call us today to review your comprehensive health care strategy (888) ARCADIA, or visit us online at www.railsofsteel.com.

CHAPTER SEVEN

Inflation

"Inflation is as violent as a mugger, as frightening as an armed robber and as deadly as a hit man."

–Ronald Reagan

We've covered a lot of ground. Between addressing income and health care needs, it might seem like we've nailed this whole retirement planning thing.

For our next stop, let's reminisce about our grandparents or even great grandparents—fonts of wisdom and life lessons. When my grandfather regaled us with tales of his childhood, he'd tell us things like, "in my day, a ticket to the movies cost a dime, a Coke cost a nickel and a penny would fill a bag of candy to the brim!"

Today, loose change is more nuisance than necessity. This is a valuable reminder of the power of inflation—the phenomenon by which goods and services get more expensive with each passing year. Some people see inflation as nothing more than a novelty, marking the passage of time. For others, inflation is an incredible burden. The difference in outlook often depends on whether your income has kept pace with inflation over time.

The effect of inflation can be small or insignificant if income is rising at the same or a greater rate. But when income is stagnant, as is often the case in retirement, then inflation can seriously erode your purchasing power, your lifestyle and your confidence. At times inflation can pack a wallop; *real* inflation between 1917 and 1920 caused prices to almost double in just three years!

Inflation doesn't typically take its toll quickly or violently, but rather more insidiously over time. Consider that the historical rate of inflation in the U.S. has been about 3 percent. That doesn't seem too bad, until you do the math!

Consider a hypothetical pensioner scheduled to collect $3,000 per month from their former employer at retirement. Assume they'll also receive $2,000 per month from Social Security. They're feeling pretty good, because their current monthly expenses are only $4,000 per month. They're scheduled to have $1,000 extra every month. What's there to worry about?

While Social Security gets a cost-of-living adjustment over time, many pensions and other retirement income sources don't. If we apply this to our case study, and assume 3 percent annual inflation, it's only 10 years before our retiree's budget is in jeopardy.

Inflation and Income				
Age	Pension	Soc. Sec.	Expenses	Difference
65	$ 3,000	$ 2,000	-$ 4,000	$ 1,000
66	$ 3,000	$ 2,030	-$ 4,120	$ 910
67	$ 3,000	$ 2,060	-$ 4,244	$ 817
68	$ 3,000	$ 2,091	-$ 4,371	$ 720
69	$ 3,000	$ 2,123	-$ 4,502	$ 621
70	$ 3,000	$ 2,155	-$ 4,637	$ 517
71	$ 3,000	$ 2,187	-$ 4,776	$ 411
72	$ 3,000	$ 2,220	-$ 4,919	$ 300
73	$ 3,000	$ 2,253	-$ 5,067	$ 186
74	$ 3,000	$ 2,287	-$ 5,219	$ 68
75	$ 3,000	$ 2,321	-$ 5,376	-$55
76	$ 3,000	$ 2,356	-$ 5,537	-$181
77	$ 3,000	$ 2,391	-$ 5,703	-$312
78	$ 3,000	$ 2,427	-$ 5,874	-$447
79	$ 3,000	$ 2,464	-$ 6,050	-$587
80	$ 3,000	$ 2,500	-$ 6,232	-$731

Inflation is like a sneaky retirement thief. Being clever, it doesn't rob you all at once. No, that would make the crime too obvious. Instead, it erodes the value of your dollars a little at a time, bit-by-bit, year-by-year. The effect of inflation can be draining and depressing if you don't have a strategy to combat it.

Inflation and the Rule of 72

If we accept that inflation is at least 3 percent then something that costs $1.00 today will cost $1.03 next year. If we instead believe that inflation is closer to 6 percent then something that costs $1.00 today will cost $1.06 next year. It's a noticeable difference, but seemingly negligible. But over decades, the impact is more pronounced. To estimate the difference, I like to use one of my favorite party tricks: the Rule of 72.

> **The Rule of 72:** Divide an anticipated rate of growth into 72 and the quotient represents how often the thing you are measuring will double. It's great for a quick-and-easy approximation. If pinpoint accuracy is essential, turn to more sophisticated analysis.
>
> 72 ÷ Growth Rate % = Doubling Time in Years

How does the Rule of 72 work? It has something to do with logarithms—a subject better tackled by your friendly neighborhood math geek. The good news is that you don't have to understand how a tool works to get some use from it (seriously...I've been using a calculator for years, but don't ask me how it works). Confused? Here's an illustration:

If your oil bill increases 3 percent each year, the cost of oil will double in 24 years. (72 ÷ 3 = 24) But if the oil bill increases by 6 percent each year, the cost will double in only 12 years! (72 ÷ 6 = 12) Got it? That's a remarkable difference, and the impact can be stunning, especially for some of retirement's more burdensome expenses like health care.

If inflation is...	Prices will double in...
2%	36 years
3%	24 years
4%	18 years
5%	14 years
6%	12 years

In the previous chapter we suggested that a married couple could expect to pay about $12,000 per year in health care costs. If a couple retires at 66 and healthcare inflation averages 3 percent, their healthcare costs will double by the time they reach age 90. However, if healthcare costs inflate by 6 percent, as is expected by some measures, then costs would *quadruple* over the same period! [57]

It's imperative we account for inflation when planning for retirement. Otherwise we risk our expenses running ahead of our income.

Inflation Rate: The Great Debate

The government has provided a measure of inflation known as the Consumer Price Index (CPI) since 1919. CPI is calculated by measuring the cost of a fixed basket of commonly purchased goods: produce, clothing, utilities and much more.

Cost-of-living adjustments (COLAs) applied to pensions, Social Security and inflation-protected securities are based on changes to the CPI. In other words, as costs rise, we rightfully expect our income to follow suit. These adjustments are our primary defense against inflation, so it's critical that CPI be calculated accurately.

The accuracy of CPI measurement is the subject of some debate, primarily concerning whether the government models are unbiased. In the early 1990s, due to mounting pressures from expanding federal deficits, Congress began exploring ways to reduce spending without having to make budget cuts. Since the CPI directly affects the cost of Social Security, our largest Federal expenditure, it found itself in the crosshairs. Shortly thereafter, the Bureau of Labor Statistics began massaging the way it calculates CPI.

The evidence can be observed in reviewing Social Security's COLA history. Between 1975 and 1990 COLAs averaged 5.9 percent, but from 1990 to 2000 the average dropped to 3.5 percent. Since 2000, COLAs have averaged just 2.2 percent. And it gets worse! Since 2009, following the last big market crash, COLAs have

---

[57] Barron's. "Healthcare Inflation Looking Ugly." June 16, 2017. http://www.barrons.com/articles/healthcare-inflation-looking-ugly-1497641776.

averaged just 1.1 percent. And can you spot the three years where Social Security recipients received no COLA at all?[58]

Cost-of-Living Adjustments to Social Security

Year	COLA	Year	COLA	Year	COLA	Year	COLA
1977	6.4	1987	1.3	1997	2.9	2007	3.3
1978	5.9	1988	4.2	1998	2.1	2008	2.3
1979	6.5	1989	4.0	1999	1.3	2009	5.8
1980	9.9	1990	4.7	2000	2.5	2010	0.0
1981	14.3	1991	5.4	2001	3.5	2011	0.0
1982	11.2	1992	3.7	2002	2.6	2012	3.6
1983	7.4	1993	3.0	2003	1.4	2013	1.7
1984	3.5	1994	2.6	2004	2.1	2014	1.5
1985	3.5	1995	2.8	2005	2.7	2015	1.7
1986	3.1	1996	2.6	2006	4.1	2016	0.0

See if you can find a retiree who agrees with the government's soft stance on inflation. The costs of energy, food and especially health care have been exploding. When you're on a fixed income you'll quickly find yourself highly sensitive to price increases. Every additional dollar spent on necessities is one less dollar available to spend on leisure, vacations or family.

In defense of the Bureau of Labor Statistics, modeling economic data such as inflation is extremely difficult. Any model containing more than a few variables risks being flawed from the outset. Measuring the price of goods, consumer sentiment and spending habits across an entire economy is a computational nightmare. But the results of this work are so influential and it's a shame to feel like the numbers are working against us.

We might not be able to control these mechanisms but we can plan around them. We know that if your income doesn't keep pace

---

[58] Social Security Administration. 2017. "Cost-of-Living Adjustment (COLA)." https://www.ssa.gov/news/cola/.

with inflation your standard of living may suffer. ,
their dependence on the CPI, pensions, Social Sec
annuities probably won't offset inflation over time.
"inflation-fighting" investments such as Treasur
tected Securities (TIPS), bonds and CDs are not cutting it because
of low interest rates or dependence on government data. It's time
to bring in the big guns.

A True Inflation Fighter

Did you think we'd make it through an entire book on retirement planning without circling back to the stock market? Not
likely!

Let's dispel any confusion. Much of this book has cast a cynical
eye on our financial future while espousing a safety-first mentality.
It's precisely because we've been so cautious, considering annuities,
pensions and Social Security for guaranteed lifetime income, and
taking separate measures to protect against healthcare costs, that
many of us can confidently take a position in risk-oriented assets.

If a market crash can no longer force us back to work or set back
our retirement budget, we can use some of the remaining assets to
help combat inflation and complement our other retirement resources that are COLA-dependent such as pensions, annuities, Social Security and other inflation-sensitive investments.

Lately, the stock market has been increasingly volatile. The soar-
ing, seemingly endless bull markets of the 80s and 90s have been
replaced by the whipsaw volatility that has marked the new millennium. Despite this frustrating transition, I believe that investing in
capital markets still offers the opportunity for the highest returns,
if you are willing to assume the risk.

At times, you will lose money with this approach; market risk is
evergreen. Given its history, it's likely you'll witness several major
market corrections over the course of your retirement. But it's pre-

.sely because of this risk that capital markets can produce big returns over time. Obviously, there are no guarantees, and you could lose money over the long-term as well, depending on your investment choices and strategy.

You don't need to put your faith entirely in the market to provide income. Instead, consider the stock market for what it has always done best: *beating inflation over time.* It's a hedge.

The Secret

Everyone wants to know how to outperform the market or find an edge. I believe the strategy for long-term market success is simple and has been well known for more than five decades:

- **Diversify.**
- **Mind your fees.**
- **And walk away.**

Too much meddling spoils the best-laid plans.

I recently had dinner with a friend who works for a big-name mutual fund company. His firm had recently conducted an internal study to learn two things: identify the investors who received the best rate of return over the previous decade and discover the secret to their success. Was it fancy website tools, the advisory help desk or the quality of their fund lineup that contributed most?

The results were entirely unexpected. When asked what contributed most to their success, an overwhelming number of respondents replied, "I forgot I even had that account!"

When it comes to long-term investing, fortune favors not the bold, but the patient (even when it is accidentally so). The entire body of academic and scientific research has backed this up for decades. After all, investments primarily go bad for two reasons: you were wrong altogether or bad timing. If you're willing to be patient, you'll have a clear advantage as timing risk shouldn't be as much of a problem.

Let's give Warren Buffett, the billionaire oracle of Omaha, the last word, *"Our favorite holding period is forever."*

Active Funds — How (Not) to Invest

When deciding how to invest for the long-term, you certainly have no shortage of options. You can buy individual stocks or bonds, mutual funds, options, exchange-traded funds (ETFs), commodities, futures ... the list goes on and on. Most investors don't have the time or expertise to dabble in the markets on their own. Inevitably, many retirees end up trusting their nest eggs to mutual funds.

Active mutual funds pool investment dollars from hundreds or thousands of investors, allowing them to share in the spoils of a common portfolio deployed under the discretion of a fund manager. Active funds tout their benefits including professional management, diversification and convenience. Of course, these funds are not providing these features as a public service; they charge investors a fee.

There are about 750 mutual fund companies, such as Fidelity Investments and Vanguard Group, offering around 10,000 mutual fund products. There are many varieties of mutual fund that primarily fall under one of two headings: actively managed or passively managed. As of the end of 2016, nearly two-thirds of these funds were actively managed.[59]

The primary objective of an actively managed mutual fund is to beat its benchmark, a standard point of reference used for comparison.

For instance, to judge the merits of a large cap mutual fund that invests exclusively in large company stock, we might compare it to

---

[59] Morningstar. Jan. 11, 2017. "U.S. Investors Favored Passive Funds Over Active by a Record Margin in 2016." https://corporate.morningstar.com/US/documents/Asset-Flows/AssetFlowsJan2017.pdf.

the S&P 500 index, which is not an investment itself, but rather a measurement of the aggregate performance of the 500 largest publicly traded U.S. companies. Remember, these active funds are charging us fees, so it would be nice if convenience was accompanied by superior returns!

The next statement may come as a surprise, but I promise it's been *common knowledge* in the industry: most active mutual funds do not beat their benchmarks.

S&P Dow Jones Indices just published its annual scorecard of S&P indices versus active funds (SPIVA) and found that nearly *87 percent* of domestic equity funds failed to outperform their respective benchmarks over a 10-year period. [60]

This is disgraceful! Actively managed funds are responsible for nearly $10 trillion of retirement assets. Why are so many doing a dismal job?

Fees — Everybody is out to make a living, including mutual fund companies. Every firm employs investment managers, administrative staff, customer service, technical support, etc. The fees we pay help these companies keep the lights on, meet payroll and provide the statements and online access we demand to monitor our performance.

But while these fees provide us with convenience they also create a dilemma. The benchmarks we use for comparative purpose have no fees attached to them. When we study the S&P 500 for instance, we're simply observing how the largest 500 U.S. companies have performed in the aggregate by market weight.

If the objective of a mutual fund is to outperform a benchmark index, it must do so *inclusive* of the fees charged to investors. According to Morningstar, Inc., the average mutual fund fee has been about 1.25 percent during the past five years. If the S&P 500 goes up 12 percent, as it did in 2016, the average competing mutual fund

---

[60] Aye M. Soe and Ryan Poirier. 2016. "SPIVA U.S. Scorecard." http://us.spindices.com/documents/spiva/spiva-us-mid-year-2016.pdf.

would need to go up 13.25 percent just to match, never mind *beat* the benchmark. That's a tall task considering...

Consistently Predicting the Future Is Impossible — Variety Magazine made a bold prediction in 1955, "It'll be gone by June." It was an article about rock 'n' roll.

Let's face it: the future is uncertain. Consider our accuracy in predicting the weather, the outcome of a ballgame and yes, the direction of the stock market. We're just as often wrong as we are right. But isn't that what makes life interesting? If life were easily predictable we'd be bored silly.

Famed economist Burton Malkiel wrote in 1973 that, "a blindfolded monkey throwing darts at a newspaper's financial pages could select a portfolio that would do just as well as one carefully selected by experts."

Over the years various groups such as the Wall Street Journal and Research Affiliates have simulated Malkiel's thought experiment, using various methodologies, to pit randomly selected portfolios against those selected by so-called experts. The results have overwhelmingly demonstrated that the experts usually fare *much worse* than random selection (no monkeys were harmed during any of the experiments).

Malkiel, taking a survey of these results 30 years after making his original comment had this to say in 2009, "Sure, there are a few people who have outperformed the index. But you can almost count them on one hand."

Beating the market consistently requires superpowers of prediction, which most mere mortals could only dream of possessing. Anyone claiming this ability is probably kidding themselves...and you.

Asset Bloat — Few mutual funds managers will achieve the acclaim and notoriety of Fidelity Investment's Peter Lynch. He'd be one of the money managers counted by Malkiel as having demonstrated an uncanny ability to beat the market. Lynch famously piloted the Magellan Fund from a modest $18 million in 1977 to a whopping $13 billion by the time he departed in 1990. Twenty-six years later, in 2016, Magellan Fund is still managing $15 billion of assets. While that's still impressive, the fund hasn't been able to match the growth of its heyday since Lynch exited.

Magellan Fund is arguably struggling under the weight of its own success. Remember, to beat the market you need to buy winners and ignore losers. A super-talented mutual fund manager like Lynch, with a few million to invest, might skillfully use their intuition and execute all the right moves.

But customers will flock to this kind of success and the targeted funds end up with billions of dollars under management. With money pouring in from eager investors, funds need to expand their pool of investments to avoid concentration risk. Eventually, as the portfolio rapidly grows, the fund will begin to resemble the very index it's competing against! One study found that most stock-oriented mutual funds were really "closet indexers," meaning they basically just track the associated benchmark index.[61]

How can a mutual fund manager, saddled with fees, ever beat the benchmark it will inevitably come to mirror? At best, It's extremely difficult. According to SPIVA, only 5 percent of mutual funds investing in large-cap U.S. stocks that had a winning three-year record against the S&P 500 continued to beat the benchmark in the subsequent three years.[62]

This is the burden of asset bloat—the concept that funds become more lethargic and less likely to deliver value as we shovel more money into them. Take a gander at the options available in your 401(k) and you will inevitably find bloated, billion-dollar funds. Working with these big, brand name firms might make us feel

---

[61] Yakov Amihud and Ruslan Goyenko. The Review of Financial Studies. Jan. 22, 2013. "Mutual Fund's R2 as Predictor of Performance." https://academic.oup.com/rfs/article-abstract/26/3/667/1593350/Mutual-Fund-s-R2-as-Predictor-of-Performance.

[62] Aye M. Soe and Ryan Poirier. 2016. "SPIVA U.S. Scorecard." http://us.spindices.com/documents/spiva/spiva-us-mid-year-2016.pdf.

good; but where it really counts, annual returns, you're likely over-paying for underperformance.

> **Convenience at a Cost** — Nearly 10 percent of actively managed funds are of the "target date" variety. I believe these funds combine high fees, asset bloat and the inability to predict the future so well as to almost make it an art form.
>
> To their credit, the design of these funds is highly desirable. During a span of predetermined years, the fund's investment allocation becomes more conservative as the target date approaches. Companies marketing target date funds recommend that you choose a fund targeting your desired retirement year. So, if you were born in 1960 and plan to retire at 65, you'd elect a fund with a target date of 2025.
>
> These funds are described as putting your retirement on autopilot, since all the work is done for you and the allocation is getting "safer" over time. The sales pitch is slick. It's no wonder they're so popular. If only they were any good.
>
> In 2008, when soon-to-be retirees desperately needed the protection of their target date funds, the most conservative of the bunch, those designed to produce income, fell an average of 17 percent. Not even one posted a positive return and the worst offender lost 41.3 percent.[63] Given this record think twice before trusting your retirement to a target date fund.

The dismal performance of actively managed mutual funds is an open secret. Every industry professional has access to the information we just covered. Why isn't this common knowledge amongst the investing public?

Marketing — Mutual fund ads are everywhere: television, magazines, online and more. What do these ads attempt to communicate? Usually that the fund companies are bastions of integrity, prestige, pedigree and excellence. Behold the mahogany furniture

---

[63] Robert Powell. MarketWatch. Feb. 4, 2009. "Target-Date Funds Missed the Target in 2008." http://www.marketwatch.com/story/questions-arise-target-date-funds-after.

and the amazing views from the corner office of a towering sky-scraper. Beaming couples nod at the sage advice delivered by a handsome advisor in a bespoke suit, just before the ad cuts to the blissful couple standing at the prow of a sailboat drifting into the sunset. They usually have sweaters tied around their necks, too. What's up with that?

What you'll seldom hear from the satin-voiced narrator is anything about performance, cost or any good reason *why* you should use their service. Who cares about that when they've got fancy slow-motion shots of smiling couples walking together down the beach? All this marketing is big on style and short on substance.

Some people mistakenly believe that these companies wouldn't be *allowed* to advertise unless they were good. How hopelessly naïve! Lousy products are marketed constantly. Look at fast food, breakfast cereals or weight-loss pills. Financial products are no different.

Illusion of Choice: Americans primarily have their retirement money socked away in 401(k) plans administered by their employer. As part of their fiduciary responsibilities, employers are made to offer enough options to satisfy the portfolio building needs of just about any investor. Whether you're young or old, conservative or aggressive, an experienced investor or a greenhorn, there are supposed to be enough choices for you to build the portfolio that's right for you. Most employers offer a broad array of mutual funds for this purpose.

Wait a second. It's your money. Why can't you invest in whatever you want?

Left to your own discretion, you might prefer a mutual fund not on the menu. Or maybe you'd prefer investing in individual stocks, a business, a piece of rental real estate or gold coins. Considering the thousands of investment opportunities available, your employer's limited menu of mutual funds, money market and target date options begins to feel awfully restrictive.

The 401(k) is really the bastard child of the incestuous relationship between Wall Street, its K Street lobbyists and Congress. It's a Frankenstein's monster of rules, regulations and conditions to which employers must adhere strictly if they want any of the special tax write-offs. I believe the regulatory requirements associated with 401(k) administration make allowance for employee investment discretion next to impossible—so it's ignored.

Active Assessment — This is not to say that actively managed funds haven't helped your nest egg grow. I'm sure many readers have watched their accounts accumulate by leaps and bounds over the last few years on the back of active fund investments. But the point is that you may have done *even better* had you used an alternative set of tools.

Passive Funds — If You Can't Beat 'Em, Join 'Em

To be fair, many of us would benefit from professional money management if it could be made to work efficiently. We all have our own work, hobbies, commitments and family obligations. That doesn't leave a lot of time to build the expertise necessary to successfully manage an investment portfolio.

Investing can be intimidating, complicated and time consuming. The average investor wants and needs professional help. But professionals aiming to beat the market have failed miserably in the aggregate. Fortunately, there's an alternative.

In 1951 a senior at Princeton University wrote a thesis arguing that mutual funds "could make no claim of superiority over market averages." His stirring assessment earned him a job at Wellington Management, a prominent money management firm at that time, where he was challenged to find a way to provide added value for investors.

Unsurprisingly, he struggled. **Why, he wondered, are we charging investors a fee to beat the market when time and again we fail in the pursuit? If we can't beat the market, why not offer investors a simple and convenient way to buy broadly into the market at minimal cost?**

This man was John Bogle. If you don't recognize the name, you're probably at least familiar with the firm he launched in 1975 to bring his investment philosophy to the public: The Vanguard Group.

Vanguard was the first professional money management firm to humble itself by making no claim of being able to beat the market. Instead, it sought to provide investors an opportunity to *participate* in the market at a conveniently low price. The Vanguard 500 Index Fund was the first passive index fund in the world, uniquely offering investors a way to participate in the market without burdensome cost overlays.

The financial collapse of 2008 erased the confidence that many investors had with their active fund managers. Since that time, a record $200 billion has shifted out of actively managed funds to passively managed funds. Vanguard now boats over $4 *trillion* dollars of assets under management, making it larger than Fidelity and TIAA combined!

Vanguard isn't the sole beneficiary of this shift. Other passively-oriented fund families, notably Dimensional Fund Advisors, iShares, SPDR Funds and others, have grown tremendously due to their success in providing new and innovative ways to bring value to the passive philosophy while keeping costs low.

Passive investing offers three distinct advantages:

Cost — The average passive fund is charging just 0.20 percent annually, about one-fifth of the going rate for an actively managed fund.

Tax-Efficiency — When it matters, the buy-and-hold styling of passive funds generates less taxable activity.

Performance — A study conducted by the faculty of the University of Pennsylvania's Wharton School found that passive index funds trumped the performance of actively managed large-cap and mid-cap funds 97 percent of the time over a 10-year period![64]

Lower fees and the potential for better performance are the one-two punch combination thrown by passive managers to put their active counterparts down on the canvas. These seemingly small differences matter in a big way. Assume for a moment that passive investing reduces your fees by 1 percent and delivers or performance, providing an additional 1 percent in returns. That could mean 2 percent or more in your pocket every year. Over time that adds up in a big way!

The difference 2% makes on a $1MM investment			
Time Period	**@ 7% Interest**	**@ 9% Interest**	**Difference**
10 years	$1,967,151	$2,367,364	20.3%
20 years	$3,869,684	$5,604,411	44.8%
30 years	$7,612,255	$13,267,678	74.2%

[64] Wharton University of Pennsylvania. 2017. "Active vs. Passive Investing: Which Approach Offers Better Returns?" http://executiveeducation.wharton.up-enn.edu/thought-leadership/wharton-wealth-management-initiative/wmi-thought-leadership/active-vs-passive-investing-which-approach-offers-better-returns.

Obviously, this information is (again) based on past performance, and I am not suggesting that passive funds will always beat active funds. But it would serve you well to explore the value that passive investing might provide for your retirement plan.

Passive Pondered — There's just one thing to remember. Passive investing is like purchasing the cheapest ticket to the rollercoaster. When the market is surging, passive investing is a good way to participate in those gains at the lowest overall cost. But when the market is crashing, you'll lose roughly the same kind of money as other investors, albeit at bargain basement prices.

For the part of your portfolio dedicated to the long term, passive investing is a good choice for many. But it also requires a certain mental toughness to stick to a passive investment strategy, especially when the going gets tough. Straying from this path has consequences.

Passive vs. Active — The Dilemma

On the surface, passive investing seems like a no-brainer. Everyone can benefit from lower fees and the potential for better performance. If only things were so cut and dry.

Consider this conundrum: while passively managed funds have outperformed actively managed funds in the aggregate, some research shows that active fund investors might be outperforming passive fund investors. How can that be possible?

Intuitively, passive fund investors tend to be more diligent and involved with their money management. They've taken some time to get educated and have identified the value that passive investing can provide as compared to active investing. But being more involved has a decidedly human consequence—the portfolios of these more proactive investors are vulnerable to emotional, irrational behaviors.

To wit, passive fund investors display an awful habit of straying from one of the foundational principles of investing success: buy low, sell high. Specifically, a 2016 study by Dalbar titled "Quantitative Analysis of Investor Behavior" found that passive investors, more so than active investors, tend to sell at the wrong times (selling low...ouch).

Annualized Investor Returns			
Period ending 12/31/16	Actively Managed	Passively Managed	Active Advantage
15 years	4.04%	2.85%	1.19%
10 years	4.37%	4.37%	0.00%
5 years	8.51%	8.12%	0.39%
3 years	3.66%	5.40%	-1.74%
1 year	6.73%	9.38%	-2.65%
Data source: Dalbar's 2016 Quantitative Analysis of Investor Behavior			

Over longer periods of time, an unsettling truth emerges: some investors lack the stomach needed to stick with a long-term strategy. It's human nature: we're prone to panic when the fruits of our labor, our retirement nest egg, is being threatened.

Clearly then, *some* defensive maneuvering, which can only be provided by active management, might be of value.

Back to Active — The Search for Value

When observing investment portfolios, you can't avoid those pretty pie charts. This eye-candy is the dumbing down of modern portfolio theory—the most influential force governing investment selection yet devised.

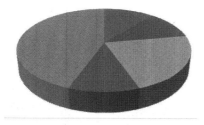

For this story, let's turn to another graduate student in search of a thesis. Harry Markowitz, a student at the University of Chicago took the advice of a friend and decided to study the stock market. More precisely, he wanted to determine how a portfolio should be constructed to maximize return for a given amount of risk. His initial findings were published in 1952. Ultimately, his research earned the Nobel Prize in Economics in 1990 and has been tremendously influential to amateur and professional money managers around the world.

Markowitz posited that investors have three primary tools at their disposal when building a portfolio: asset allocation, market timing and individual investment selection.

Asset allocation is the endeavor to diversify across various investment categories, in measured proportions, to achieve a target return over time. Categories include stocks, bonds, cash, commodities, real estate, etc.

Market timing represents short-term deviations from this plan, such as shifting between asset categories or getting in or out of the market, to take advantage of short-term trends.

Individual investment selection refers to the specific choices you make to represent an asset category. For example, if you decided your portfolio needed to hold large cap stock, you could accomplish this by purchasing shares of stock in individual companies. Alternatively, you might instead elect to participate in a mutual fund.

Countless studies have been conducted to determine which of these tools exerts the greatest influence on portfolio success. One of the most influential, *Determinants of Portfolio Performance*, was published in 1986. It concluded that more than 93 percent of portfolio variance is determined by the strength of asset allocation alone, with market timing and quality of individual investment selection having less than 7 percent influence.[65]

The mutual fund industry latched onto this work and used it to bolster its marketing outreach over the past three decades. Pie charts peacocking broad diversification became the visual of choice and "set it and forget it" the rallying cry. The power of diversification strengthens the argument in favor of passive investing. If asset allocation is so influential, what possible room is there for an active manager to add additional value?

Against all odds, there *is* room for improvement! Another study, published in 2010 and titled *The Equal Importance of Asset Allocation and Active Management*, criticized the work published 25 years earlier. The authors argued that, while asset allocation is of course very influential, the original analysis did not adjust for market momentum.[66] The argument was simple: if a rising tide lifts all boats, it may be more critical just to get your boat in the water as opposed to fussing about which harbor to use!

The authors found that roughly 75 percent of a portfolio's return comes from general market movement, with the remaining portion split roughly between asset allocation and active management. **The**

---

[65] Gary P. Brinson, L. Randolph Hood, and Gilbert L. Beebower. Financial Analysts Journal. 1969. "Determinants of Portfolio Performance." ftp://139.82.198.57/mgarcia/Seminario/textos_preliminares/100331%20brinson_Determinants_Portfolio_Performance.pdf.

[66] James X. Xiong, Roger G. Ibbotson, Thomas M. Idzorek and Peng Chen. Financial Analysts Journal. 2010. "The Equal Importance of Asset Allocation and Active Management." https://corporate.morningstar.com/ib/documents/MethodologyDocuments/IB-BAssociates/EqualImportanceOfAssetAllocActiveMgmt.pdf.

big takeaway is that *just being invested in the first place* could be the greatest determinant in achieving long-term rate of return success. However, there is still *substantial* room for proactivity to add value.[67] But we've already discussed how many money managers fail in their quest to provide this additional value. Can it be done?

Finding *Alpha* — Markowitz influenced investors worldwide to use asset allocation as the primary driver of portfolio design. Today, this style of portfolio management is known as strategic asset allocation (SAA), which holds that investors should deploy their assets amongst a risk-targeted allocation, making only minor adjustments to keep the portfolio on track over time.

An alternative school of thought attempts to enhance this model. It's called tactical asset allocation (TAA). The argument is that a portfolio can be dynamically managed from time to time to take advantage of systematic and global trends, inefficiencies, temporary imbalances or shifts in the market. Here's a good way to think of it: SAA focuses on building a strong foundation while TAA attempts to add value on the margins.

This is where it gets tricky. Not all TAA strategists are successful, but even when they are we know that past performance is not indicative of future returns. Because the future is so difficult to predict, proactive or complicated market-timing strategies tend to produce mixed results. **But a very select group of tactical managers have had phenomenal track records of earning excess return relative to the benchmark (known as *alpha*). In some cases, they might also demonstrate a history of mitigating downside risk.**

We prefer TAA strategists that seek alpha through *combining* the respective strengths of passive and active management. Consider that some asset classes, like large cap domestic stocks or short-term

---

[67] As with all investing strategies, neither asset allocation nor diversification can ensure a profit or guarantee that you won't lose money.

U.S. government bonds, are more straightforward. There is a limited pool of investment options, which all tend to perform similarly over time, so why employ an active manager when there is little room to provide *alpha*? Instead, passive strategies might make more sense, allowing you to participate in these sectors at the lowest overall cost.

But a properly allocated investment portfolio could require exposure to more complicated asset classes such as real estate, small cap stock or international markets. Investment options here tend to be more diverse and performance between individual options can vary wildly. Here, active managers can deploy a host of tools to cull the weak and keep us exposed to the better investment options. This is your portfolio's opportunity to capture *alpha*; the key is to identify and utilize those few active managers who have demonstrated a proficiency in navigating their respective asset class.

Undoubtedly, the investor public will continue to debate which is superior: active or passive management. We've simply concluded that both styles have their pros and cons, so there is ample room to use both. The money managers we recommend embrace this philosophy by combining exposure to active and passive management. The endeavor is for the strengths of these two investment styles to work together in overcoming their respective weaknesses. We believe this is the best way to help our clients mitigate downside risk while seeking superior risk-adjusted returns.

Ultimately, if we're going to effectively combat inflation over time, it will require the patience to stick with a long-term strategy. Designing and understanding a well-deployed investment portfolio may give you the confidence necessary to stay the course, especially when the going gets tough.

Connecting the Dots

Back in college, a roommate returned from winter break with a thought-provoking story. He'd been cleaning out his desk at home and came across a stack of old birthday cards. He was taking a moment to read through the old mementos when out from one card fluttered a $10 bill.

The card was from an aunt—they were both big movie buffs. Every year they would see a summer blockbuster together and the money was meant to cover their tickets, popcorn and soda. For whatever reason, they never went to the movies that year. He planned on giving his aunt a call, to tell her of the discovery and plan that long overdue date, but lamented with a little tongue-in-cheek that the $10 would now barely purchase one movie ticket...never mind two with snacks to boot!

Idle money left in the bank, a desk drawer or under the mattress is never truly "safe". True, the dollars themselves are preserved, but inflation robs them of precious purchasing power over time. To preserve the real value of your savings, some of your dollars will need to be positioned to match or beat inflation over time.

Withdrawals from an investment portfolio can bridge the gap when increases to your cost-of-living aren't matched by increases to your guaranteed income. Being that withdrawals for this purpose should be much smaller in the short-term, it should provide you and the portfolio the patience necessary to fearlessly invest for the long term.

ON-TRACK INFLATION FOCUS

Have you measured the potential, long-term impact of inflation on your retirement plan? Are you comfortable with your current portfolio? Have you measured how much risk you're taking or how much you're paying in fees?

Call us today to review your inflation fighting strategy (888) AR-CADIA, or visit us online at www.railsofsteel.com.

CHAPTER EIGHT

Taxes

"In this world, nothing can be said to be certain, except death and taxes."
—Benjamin Franklin

Few would challenge the wisdom of Benjamin Franklin, but retirees repeat a different mantra as though they were exempt from his maxim, "I'll be in a lower tax bracket in retirement, so what's there to worry about?"

Apart from housing expenses and healthcare costs, few things cause more pain in retirement than the income you'll be separated from by taxation. We're going to cover the myriad tax issues that await an unexpecting retiree and, more importantly, review techniques that help avoid these mistakes.

Tax-Deferral: The Great Deceit

Every April, millions of Americans go through the lengthy, expensive and arduous process of filing their tax return. It doesn't matter if you have an accountant, use do-it-yourself software or crunch through the paperwork with a pencil, inevitably you find yourself somewhat disgruntled. Though former Vice President Joe Biden once described paying taxes as a great act of patriotism, most Americans spare no effort to reduce their share of the collective burden by any legal means possible.

Every year, as filers desperately seek solace, they encounter a timeless piece of advice proffered by just about every tax advisor, "looking to reduce your bill or increase your refund? Just add more money to your 401(k) or IRA. It will *reduce* your taxable income and *save* you a bunch!" By the millions, Americans dutifully act upon this advice and shuttle hard-earned dollars into their retirement plans, taking comfort in having saved on their taxes. If only it were that simple!

The IRS classifies 401(k) plans, IRAs and most other retirement accounts as tax-deferred. Words have meaning, people. Something that is tax-deferred means you get to skip the taxes now ... only to pay them later! Withdrawals from these accounts in retirement are taxed in their entirety as ordinary income.

Tax deferral can have its benefits. Some investments will accrue more value in the absence of current taxation. But it's time you paid closer attention to your future tax liabilities.

What Happened to My Lower Tax Bracket?

Many mistakenly believe they'll be in a lower tax bracket when they retire, softening the impact taxes will have on their savings and income. Unfortunately, this is sometimes wishful thinking. If you're assuming you'll be paying less tax in retirement because you'll be earning less income, think again.

Consider your salary strongly influences the lifestyle you enjoy today. Chances are, you'll want your retirement income to be comparable, so that you won't have to make many changes to your lifestyle. Many retirees want their retirement income to be as close to their working income as possible.

And what typically replaces that working income? Social Security? Some of that benefit can get taxed as ordinary income. Pension? Ditto—taxed as ordinary income. Withdrawals from 401(k) or IRAs? The same. In fact, nearly all sources of retirement income are taxed as ordinary income, no different than if you had earned that money in a paycheck! Worse yet, most folks' biggest tax deductions, mortgage interest and dependents, are typically gone or substantially reduced at this point in your life.

And what of the future? Consider what you think tax rates will look like 10, 20 or even 30 years from now. Do you think tax rates will go up or down? This country is nearly $20 trillion dollars in debt. There are only two options for eradicating debt: spend less or tax more.

What have you observed as Washington's remedy of choice? In the near term, a Trump presidency may lead to lower tax rates. But the pendulum will swing several times between liberals and conservatives over the course of your retirement. Chances are that tax rates could go up, perhaps markedly so, somewhere along that stretch.

At times, tax rates in this country have been substantially higher. In 1944, to address the debt associated with engaging in the Second World War, the highest marginal tax rate was 94 percent! With our national debt now exceeding *20 trillion dollars*, isn't it reasonable to suspect that higher rates are at least a possibility?

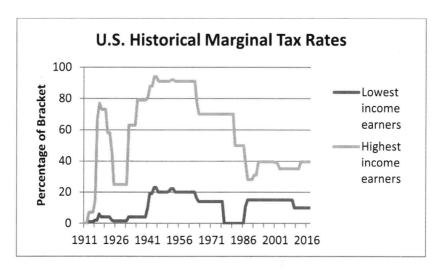

Insult to Injury

The taxes you'll pay in retirement are also directly related to penalties that may apply to your Social Security and Medicare benefits. Once taxable income exceeds a certain level, as much as 85 percent of your Social Security benefits become taxable and Medicare premiums can increase with the addition of surcharges.

Social Security Taxation — Wait a minute. Your Social Security benefit was funded through taxes paid by you and your employer while you were working. Yet, when you receive this benefit, it can be taxed? You better believe it.

> **Provisional Income:** Determining if your Social Security benefit is taxable requires calculating your "provisional income." Here's how to do it:
>
> Start with your modified adjusted gross income (MAGI). Add the value of any tax-exempt interest received for the year, such as that from municipal bonds. Finally, add 50 percent of your Social Security benefits to the total. Written as a formula:
>
> MAGI + Tax Exempt Interest + 50% of Social Security = Provisional Income

Find your marital status and provisional income in the following table to determine what amount of your Social Security benefits will be taxable:

Taxes on Social Security		
Filing Status	Provisional Income	Social Security Taxation
Single/Head of Household	Less than $25,000	0%
	$25,000 to $34,000	Up to 50%
	More than $34,000	Up to 85%
Joint Filers	Less than $32,000	0%
	$32,000 to $44,000	Up to 50%
	More than $44,000	Up to 85%

It doesn't take much for your Social Security benefits to be taxable at the highest level. Did you notice that tax-free municipal bonds, something retirees specifically invest in to *avoid* taxation, count against you?

Medicare Surcharge — To make matters worse, too much income is punished by way of having to pay significantly more for Medicare Parts B and D. To calculate your exposure, add your MAGI to any tax-exempt interest. Compare your number to the corresponding figure in the following table.

Medicare Surcharges Adjusted Gross Income + Tax-Exempt Interest			
Single Filer Income	Joint Filer Income	Part B Premium	Part D Surcharge
Up to $85,000	Up to $170,000	$134 or average $190	--
$85,001 to $107,000	$170,001 to $214,000	$187.50	$13.30
$107,001 to $160,000	$214,001 to $320,000	$267.90	$34.20
$160,001 to $214,000	$320,001 to $428,000	$348.30	$55.20
More than $214,000	More than $428,000	$428.60	$76.2

Unintended Consequences

Not long ago I met with a man who was widowed after his wife's tragic passing several years earlier. His wife was clearly the love of his life and the loss affected him deeply.

In his grief, he took a substantial withdrawal from his IRA to purchase an historic home. Being good with his hands, he figured a major renovation project would provide plenty distraction.

He was aware that the IRA withdrawal would be paired with a hefty tax bill the following year. What he wasn't expecting was that same transaction subjected him to the maximum Medicare surcharge for the next two years, costing him thousands more.

There's a lesson to be learned here. We can naively believe that every transaction has a simple and straightforward tax consequence. But given the size and scope of the US tax code, it might be safer to assume that every transaction may have two or three unintended consequences. Having a qualified financial advisor as a resource can help these headaches.

Don't Forget About RMDs — Another unpleasant tax event is forced upon your tax-deferred accounts when you reach age 70 ½. The IRS compels you to take a required minimum distribution (RMD)—a forced withdrawal that exposes these savings to taxation. Being tax-deferred, these savings may have avoided taxation for years, maybe decades. But come age 70 ½ your Uncle Sam is through being patient; he wants those tax dollars!

RMDs are mandatory. Fail to comply and the IRS assesses a penalty amounting to 50 percent of what you should have withdrawn. That's a stiff price to pay, don't forget to take your RMDs!

The RMD is calculated as a percentage of the previous year-end balance for all tax-deferred accounts. Many people are surprised to learn that the percentage you're required to withdraw increases every year!

IRS Uniform Lifetime Table (for calculating RMDs)							
Age	%	Age	%	Age	%	Age	%
70	3.65	81	5.59	93	10.42	104	20.40
71	3.77	82	5.85	94	10.99	105	22.22
72	3.91	83	6.13	95	11.63	106	23.81
73	4.05	84	6.45	96	12.35	107	25.64
74	4.20	85	6.76	97	13.16	108	27.03
75	4.37	86	7.09	98	14.08	109	29.41
76	4.55	87	7.46	99	14.92	110	32.26
77	4.72	88	7.87	100	15.87	111	34.48
78	4.93	89	8.33	101	16.95	112	38.46
79	5.13	90	8.77	102	18.18	113	41.67
80	5.35	91	9.25	103	19.23	114	47.61
		92	9.80			115	52.63

Many retirees fail to include the impact of RMDs on their retirement income and unwittingly walk into those Social Security and Medicare penalties when retirement is long under way. **In some cases, your RMD obligations may be so large as to risk exposing you to even higher tax brackets.**

Widow's Wallop — Consider that if you're married, you may one day survive your spouse. Most retirees are familiar with the fact that as a survivor you'll lose one of the Social Security checks, albeit the smaller of the two.

The more insidious surprise the government has in store is that the IRS will henceforth require the survivor to file their taxes as a *single* taxpayer. The tax rates for single filers are substantially higher than those for married filers. Without having done planning in advance, many survivors have no choice but to take the tax increase on the chin.

The Bottom Line — Over the years, many people have solely focused on finding tax breaks for their previous year's tax return. This often leads toward overweighting retirement savings into tax-deferred positions, despite the detrimental consequences this might have further down the road in retirement. It's time to get serious about managing your future tax obligations.

The Tax-Control Triangle

The federal government effectively has three primary ways to tax your retirement savings, depending on how the money has been stored. The tax-control triangle helps visualize these methods:

TAX-FAVORED

- Roth IRA⁸
- Municipal Bond⁴
- Cash Value Life Insurance¹

Investments are made after taxes with any growth generally tax deferred. Municipal bond interest, Roth IRA distributions, life insurance death benefits are generally income tax free. Life insurance cash value distributions and loans are tax free.

TAXABLE

- Cash
- Checking
- CDs
- Money Market
- Non-Qualified Brokerage

These dollars are invested after tax and every year the owner receives a 1099 form for any interest/dividends earned. This category is beneficial for it's high liquidity.

TAX-DEFERRED

- 401 (k)/403 (b)
- Traditional IRAs
- SEP/SIMPLE
- Pension
- Qualified Retirement Plans

These dollars typically provide tax-deductible contributions and tax-deferred growth, but upon distribution, are taxed as ordinary income.

Tax-Deferred

Most retirement savers are intimately familiar with tax-deferred savings. We've already covered why it's so attractive to invest here. First, deferring income tax is tempting every April 15. Second, your employer may provide an incentive match for contributions into the company retirement plan, you'd be a fool to turn away the free money.

But some of the tax consequences of deferred savings are not avoided, just delayed. Once we've retired, paying too much income tax becomes a real burden, especially if it leads to penalties and surcharges on our federal benefits. And what if tax rates increase in the future? Too much tax-deferred savings can lead you directly into the various traps and pitfalls reviewed earlier. It can be of enormous benefit to use other savings options.

Taxable

The accounts and investments listed here are tax-liquid, meaning they can be spent without fear of a tax penalty. But this liquidity comes at a price: dividends and interest are taxable in the year they're received, as are capital gains at point of sale. The good news is that the applicable taxes are less onerous than income tax for most situations. Dividends and long-term capital gains tax is 15 percent for most retirees, while interest is taxable at your marginal tax rate.

These accounts are also a great home for money intended for heirs and beneficiaries. Following your death, most investments experience a "step-up in basis," which means that beneficiaries will not be taxed on the gains accrued to that point. Imagine how thrilled your heirs would be if they received the Apple stock you purchased for 21 cents in 1982!

The taxable bucket isn't perfect. It's called taxable for a reason. Every transaction can generate a taxable event, as does every dividend earned and all interest received. A good way to combat this is to have a low turnover investment strategy, meaning you'll want to engage in fewer transactions, trades and sales in any given year.

The key takeaways are that taxable accounts are not subject to RMDs, may be subject to lower taxation and may be tax-advantaged when passing to heirs.

Tax-Free

Tax-free is our last category! All distributions, if you play by the rules, come out tax-free. **This category is so powerful that the IRS imposes strict limitations on the types of accounts that qualify and how much money can be added every year.** These options deserve your attention:

Roth IRA — Introduced in 1997, the Roth IRA has become one of the more popular retirement vehicles in the country. It was incorporated into the Tax Relief Act and named for the late Senator William Roth of Delaware. The Roth IRA is popular for three good reasons:

- While it offers no tax breaks when funded, all qualifying distributions taken beyond age 59 ½ (and after the account has been open for at least 5 years) are 100 percent tax-free!
- The IRS doesn't compel withdrawals while living (no RMDs)
- The tax-free treatment extends to beneficiaries

While many people are eligible to fund a Roth IRA, it's such a powerful tax-saving tool that the IRS imposes strict limitations on contributions (see table below). First, you'll need to have earned income such as from a paycheck or commissions. Contributions are also limited and then prohibited outright at specific income levels. If these hurdles are cleared you may contribute up to $5,500 to your Roth IRA in 2017 ($6,500 for those beyond age 50).

If you want to add big bucks to a Roth IRA, you might consider executing a Roth conversion. A conversion turns a traditional IRA into a Roth IRA so that the account gains all the advantages described above. Conversion also offers high-income earners an opportunity to invest in a Roth IRA if they would otherwise be prohibited. Another option for folks in this position is to make a nondeductible traditional IRA contribution and then immediately convert it to a Roth. This is known as "backdoor" funding.

Because Roth conversions are taxed as ordinary income in the year of the conversion, the maneuver must be made carefully to avoid entering a higher tax bracket. Conversion works well for savers who want to protect their IRA from RMDs, believe tax rates may be higher in the future, find themselves in an advantageous tax situation and/or have idle funds available outside of the IRA to pay the taxes upon conversion. For example, if you were to become subject to job loss or transition, you might find yourself in a temporarily lower tax bracket, creating a potential opportunity to convert dollars tax efficiently.

Roth IRA Contribution Limits		
If your filing status is...	And your modified AGI is...	You can contribute...
married filing jointly OR qualifying widow(er)	$0 to $186,000	up to the limit
	$186,000 to $196,000	a reduced amount
	$196,000+	zero
married filing separately AND you lived with your spouse at any time during the year	$0 to $10,000	a reduced amount
	$10,000+	zero
single OR head of household OR married filing separately AND you did <u>not</u> live with your spouse at any time during the year	$0 to $118,000	up to the limit
	$118,000 to $133,000	a reduced amount
	$133,000+	zero

> ### Roth Conversions in Action
>
> **Problem:** A 60-year-old married couple is trying to save as much as possible before retirement, but they are prohibited from funding a Roth IRA because of their income level. **Potential Solution:** They can "backdoor" their way into a Roth IRA. To execute, they must first make a non-deductible traditional IRA contribution and then subsequently convert the savings to Roth IRA.
>
> **Problem:** A 62-year-old man is retiring with plenty of guaranteed income. He's also got lots of tax-deferred savings which he's hoping to leave primarily to his beneficiaries. But he knows that come age 70 ½ his RMD requirements might push him into a higher tax bracket. He's also concerned about the national debt and thinks tax rates will be higher in the future. **Potential Solution:** Our friend could consider converting some of his tax-deferred accounts to Roth IRA over the next eight years. The benefit is two-fold. Conversions done today pay the applicable tax now, mitigating the risk of potential higher tax rates in the future. The converted dollars are also exempt from RMD obligation. Arranged correctly, his future RMD exposure may be controlled to help avoid those higher tax brackets.
>
> **Problem:** A 55-year-old has just been laid off from work and is feeling dejected. She won't be able to save anything toward retirement until she returns to work. Is there anything she can do in the interim to keep retirement on track? **Potential Solution:** Turn lemons into lemonade! Job loss might place you in a temporarily lower tax bracket. This might be an opportunity to convert some tax-deferred savings to Roth IRA at a "discounted" tax rate! Furthermore, the 10% penalty that typically applies to tax-deferred distributions prior to age 59 ½ does not apply to Roth conversions.
>
> These hypothetical examples are but a few of the many ways a Roth conversion can work to your advantage. An experienced financial planner can root out what strategies might work well for your unique situation.

Municipal Bonds (Munis) — Municipal bonds have been a favorite investment for tax-sensitive retirees for more than a century. Federal, state and local governments issue bonds to raise cash for projects of all types. These municipal issuers create incentives for investors by exempting the interest on these bonds from federal or state taxation ... sometimes both. Earning tax-free interest is like having your cake and eating it, too!

The current problem with munis is their attractiveness suffers in this low-interest-rate environment. While interest may accrue tax-free, the low rates are often unable to help investors meet or beat inflation. There's also some concern regarding credit quality, as many municipalities are already struggling to make good on current, never mind future debt commitments. Munis will likely regain their popularity as interest rates climb, but should still be considered as part of a well-balanced plan.

Cash Value Life Insurance — Life insurance is like the Swiss army knife of financial products. Policies can be positioned to provide not only financial benefits for beneficiaries, but also to help with the costs of long-term medical expenses while living or even serve as a source of *tax-free* supplemental retirement income in some instances. Some life insurance contracts can combine these benefits in a single policy!

This flexibility is not to be ignored. In fact, the versatility of life insurance is what sets it apart in the tax-efficiency category, especially for people earning higher incomes. Primary benefits include:

- Death claims paid to beneficiaries are *tax-free* [68]
- There are no limitations on premiums based on income
- Cash values grow tax-deferred
- Withdrawals, taken as policy loans, are *tax-free*

Those are some amazing tax benefits. A properly positioned life insurance policy can help protect the financial interests of your family while simultaneously providing a source of tax-free retire-

---

[68] If properly structured, proceeds from life insurance are generally income tax free. Income-tax-free distributions are achieved by withdrawing to the cost basis (premiums paid), then using policy loans. Loans and withdrawals may generate an income tax liability, reduce available cash value, and reduce the death benefit, or cause the policy to lapse. This assumes the policy qualifies as life insurance and is not a modified endowment contract.

ment income using policy loans. Because there are no premium limits based on income, high-income earners can freely make larger premium payments to a life insurance policy when they might otherwise be prohibited from funding a Roth IRA. For this reason, cash value life insurance policies are sometimes referred to as the "rich man's Roth."

Systematic premiums to the policy, less the cost of insurance, earn interest in various ways depending on the product, often with enough options to appease both conservative and aggressive consumers.

Note that tax-free income is only possible for loans against the policy, not withdrawals. Loans do not need to be repaid, since you're borrowing from yourself, but the amount "owed" is deducted from the death benefit when the policy pays out. It's important that there be a permanent and legitimate need for insurance before engaging in this strategy.

Another consideration is time. It takes many years to build sufficient cash value in a life insurance policy to the point where loans can be taken without jeopardizing the integrity of the underlying protection. If this strategy is of interest, it's best to begin as early as possible. Due diligence and careful planning are necessary before leveraging this powerful strategy.

Working in Harmony

In summary, I believe too many people are blindly saving for retirement exclusively with tax-deferred accounts. This can be a grievous error as it subjects all your withdrawals to taxation and by extension to penalties, surcharges and higher tax rates.

Smart savers might make ample use of taxable and tax-free accounts to diversify their tax obligations. When you're retired, if you can pull withdrawals from all three elements of the tax-control triangle, it might be possible to suppress federal income taxation to 15 percent or less and avoid some, if not all, tax-related retirement pitfalls. Here are some good general rules to consider when diversifying your retirement tax strategy:

- Fund your employer plan as much as necessary to get every penny of what they're willing to match. After all, free money is the best kind of money!
- Want to save more? Consider making maximum contributions to a Roth IRA.
- *Still* have dollars to save? Returning to the employer plan might make sense if it will help lower your tax bracket. Otherwise, consider funding a taxable account or alternative financial vehicle.

This advice is not one-size-fits-all and is not meant as a formal recommendation to readers. All situations are different and, given how confusing tax planning can be, it's essential to do your homework. Be sure to consult with your financial advisor and qualified tax consultant to learn about all available options.

Distribution Order Matters

Readers with a penchant for baking know that technique matters. Two people might start with the same ingredients and with the same recipe, but the order in which they combine those ingredients might produce a delicious or disastrous confection (I've learned the hard way that sifting your dry ingredients before adding the wet stuff is very important).

At the precipice of retirement, you'll need to determine a withdrawal strategy. But how do you determine the order in which to withdraw your savings to minimize taxation? The answer is not as straightforward as you might think. Should you first take withdrawals from tax-deferred, taxable or tax-free accounts? Or perhaps you should be withdrawing proportionally across the three?

The conventional wisdom is to first take money from taxable accounts because these savings are already subject to tax and may qualify for advantageous capital gains treatment. Next, it's advised that withdrawals be taken from tax-deferred accounts, to delay paying the associated ordinary income tax and to benefit from tax-deferred growth. Finally, it's said that withdrawals should come from tax-free accounts to maximize what's possible for growth when unhindered from taxation.

While following this advice may be best for your situation, it could also be a recipe for inefficiency. In many cases, it doesn't make sense to delay tax-deferred withdrawals, as future RMD obligations may push you into higher tax brackets. Sometimes it makes more sense to begin taking tax-deferred withdrawals sooner, or at least consider Roth conversion.

Fortunately, there is software available that meticulously combs through the withdrawal options available for your unique situation so you can measure the best way to help reduce your tax liabilities not only now, but in the future. In some cases, the difference between paying the most or least in tax over time could amount to thousands or even millions of dollars.

The Price of Ignoring Tax

We recently met with a couple who wanted a second opinion on their financial situation just ahead of retirement. They were very confident but looking to make sure nothing was missing. Their optimism was easy to understand; the advisor they'd been working with for over a decade had helped them double their net worth since the 2008 crash.

This advisor was most definitely an adept portfolio manager. Their investments were sound, their fees were reasonable and the tremendous success they experienced in building their nest egg was exemplary.

But they were being advised to take retirement income according to conventional wisdom by first taking withdrawals from taxable accounts and then later from tax-deferred accounts. This would almost assuredly be a mistake.

It's an easy trap to fall into; taking withdrawals early on in retirement from taxable accounts is tempting since capital gains are typically taxed around 15%. But for this couple, we projected that RMD obligations down the road might force ordinary income taxation of 33% or more!

Our analysis showed that front-loading their tax obligation through Roth Conversions could keep them in the 15% tax bracket throughout the entire duration of their retirement, potentially saving them and their heirs hundreds of thousands of dollars.

There is nothing wrong with having worked with a skilled portfolio manager. But if you're relying on them navigating you through all the complications that retirement presents, think again. There's too much of your hard-earned money at stake!

The tax man is insatiable, but in many instances, he only takes what we're careless enough to feed him. The financial industry doesn't often help, at times encouraging you to focus on portfolio returns with little mind to taxation. But remember this: it's not what you make that counts, but what you keep. Do your homework and fight to keep in your pocket what's rightfully yours.

ON-TRACK TAX FOCUS

Have you taken steps to avoid Social Security and Medicare taxes, penalties and surcharges? Are you confident that your assets are taking advantage of proper tax diversification? Have you identified the most tax efficient retirement income distribution strategy?

Call us today to review your tax mitigation plan (888) ARCADIA, or visit us online at www.railsofsteel.com.

CHAPTER NINE

Estate Planning

"Death is not the end. There remains the litigation over the estate."
—Ambrose Bierce

ongratulations! If you've made it this far, you know of enough tools, and the right questions to ask, to punch   Your Ticket to Retirement. Once you've prepared adequately for your retirement needs, it's time to consider what happens to your assets should they pass to the next generation—estate planning.

Depending on its design, scope and complexity an estate plan can offer valuable protections to you and your beneficiaries including privacy, protection from creditors, guardianships, tax reduction and even defenses against the costs of long-term care.

Last wills and testaments have formed the foundation for the protection of financial interests for thousands of years. Evidence of such directives has been discovered in ancient Greece, Rome and Egypt.

Modern-day Americans appear to be decidedly less organized than their ancestors. Per a recent Gallup survey, only 44 percent of adult Americans have a will.[69] This means that most Americans could be leaving a big mess for their families. This is not only unfair, but potentially a financial disaster for the people or charities we care about most.

Dying "intestate" (without a will) guarantees your heirs will end up in court.

Probate

Contending with the loss of a loved one can be a harrowing event. Emotions are running high, arrangements need to be made and eventually concern will turn to the distribution of assets. At a time when you're probably wishing that life would just return to normal, the last thing you'll want to hear is that the distribution of assets is going to be administered by a state-presided judicial process. Welcome to probate.

Probate court has roots in English common law. The proper distribution of property following a person's death was a matter in dispute for centuries between the interests of church, state and bereaved families. Over time, the church won sovereignty over the allotment of men's souls; while the state took over the distribution of physical and financial assets.

---

[69] Jeffrey M. Jones. Gallup. May 18, 2016. "Majority in U.S. Do Not Have a Will." http://www.gallup.com/poll/191651/majority-not.aspx.

Probate court acts as an administrator, reviewing a will's legitimacy, making sure it's a valid document representing the true last testament of the deceased. Next, the court appoints an executor who is responsible for paying claims against the estate of the deceased and oversees the distribution of what remains. Finally, probate has authority over a slew of other administrative elements including:

- Publication of notices for creditors or others wishing to make a claim
- Resolving claims in dispute
- Protecting the rights of beneficiaries that may be minors or otherwise unable to speak for themselves
- Shepherding actions such as lawsuits that may arise in conjunction with the passing of the deceased or that have been underway at the time of death
- Ensuring that estate taxes, gift taxes or inheritance taxes are paid if the estate exceeds certain thresholds
- Providing guidance to the executor in how and when to distribute assets

This is by no means a comprehensive list, but it demonstrates that, despite its worthy intentions, probate opens the door to a time-consuming, protracted and potentially very expensive process.

Probate Can Get Ugly — Earlier in my career, I had a coworker who was the sole beneficiary of his deceased uncle's estate. Having never been married and with no children of his own, the uncle ignored all other family members and left everything to his nephew in his will. The uncle didn't have much: a house, a modest bank balance and a few stock certificates. But the value of these assets had the potential to make a real difference in the life of my soon-to-be-married friend.

That is, until he realized that a will *guarantees* probate. Depending on the laws of the state that hold jurisdiction, assets

in probate are usually frozen and cannot be withdrawn, transferred or sold for a period, to give creditors ample opportunity to put liens against the estate and for interested parties to contest the will. This process can take anywhere from six months to several years.

Unfortunately for my friend, it was during this period that a woman happened by the probate proceeding and declared that she was the uncle's illegitimate daughter and therefore should be sole beneficiary of the estate! The woman was unknown to any of the parties and clearly unbalanced. However, as the saying goes, everyone gets their day in court. It took nearly two years to legally discredit her claim and, by the time all was said and done, my friend spent nearly every penny of his uncle's estate on attorney's fees.

Probate is a public process during which your beneficiaries may spend thousands of dollars in court and legal fees. The most alarming aspect of probate is that a judge, an angry neighbor, the village crazy person or even the beneficiaries themselves can contest, dispute or overturn the will. An attorney once told me of his experience with two siblings who reduced an estate to nothing over their inability to agree on who should inherit a *pocket watch*! **Here's the lesson: friends don't let friends go through probate court.**

Skip It — Probate can be avoided entirely with a little planning. The easiest way, requiring no fancy or expensive legal maneuvers, is to have properly drawn beneficiary designations. Many assets such as bank accounts, IRAs, life insurance proceeds and other retirement plan accounts can be distributed without a will and skip probate altogether. However, there are exceptions; a good financial planner or attorney will point those out.

But there is risk as well. These assets may still enter probate if a beneficiary is deceased, incapacitated or a minor child without guardianship. Note that some assets cannot be granted a beneficiary designation such as physical and personal property.

Five Essential Estate Planning Documents

A collective reluctance to plan is understandable. Death is an un-comfortable topic and few, except for the philosophers among us, like dwelling on our own mortality. But you've gotten this far because you've committed to creating a plan. Prudence demands we consider the disposition of our worldly goods for the protection of our assets, our families and most importantly, ourselves.

Generally, a will by itself is just a starting point. For many, a will doesn't resolve the final distribution of your assets and risks ignoring other valuable protections. If you want better protection for the estate, you'll want to consider what I've dubbed the Five Essentials:

1. Revocable Living Trust
2. Pour-Over Will
3. Health Care Proxy and Living Will
4. Durable Financial Power of Attorney
5. Homestead Exemption

Before we explore any further, I want to comment about the time and place to begin your estate-planning journey.

When considering retirement, some people begin by arranging their estate planning affairs first. While it's admirable to protect the interests of one's beneficiaries, this is a clear example of putting the cart before the horse and can be an expensive mistake.

Retirement planning often requires changes to the structure and placement of your financial assets. If you start your planning process by drawing up a will or trusts, any changes to your financial accounts may require that those legal documents be amended. This may require a trip back to the attorney's office and incurring additional fees. You'd do better to think of the Five Essentials as the cherry on top of your retirement plan—complete this step last to help ensure minimal cost.

Revocable Living Trust

A revocable living trust is a legal entity that holds assets for the benefit of others during your lifetime. The beauty of a revocable living trust is that you, as both grantor and trustee, have complete control over the assets while living. The revocable part means you can change, add and remove assets in the trust at any time. You can also elect a successor trustee that will take over control of the trust after you pass. All assets transferred in this manner skip probate.

A revocable trust typically becomes irrevocable at death. At this point, the trustee is bound to manage and distribute the assets according to the instructions you provide. This allows you to exercise a great deal of control from beyond the grave.

For example, if one of your beneficiaries happens to be irresponsible with money, you can specify their share only be distributed under certain conditions. You might also prefer for assets to be distributed slowly over time as opposed to all at once. This may help beneficiaries stretch their inheritance, reduce their tax obligations or shelter their interests should they go through a divorce or bankruptcy.

Many people only concern themselves with *who* gets the money. But equal attention should be paid to *why* or *when*. By providing a specific set of instructions and conditions directing the trustees on how to use trust assets you can protect the interests of the beneficiaries as well as your own goals and wishes.

This is not a subject to be glossed over lightly. Inherited wealth can cause far more problems than it solves. Some beneficiaries will feel tremendous guilt or grief in receiving assets they might not feel they deserve. For others, an inheritance may cause marital issues, get lost in divorce, discourage the pursuit of career goals, make someone the target of fraud or be directed toward bad financial or business decisions. Any of these examples can leave beneficiaries in worse financial shape than they were before receiving the inheritance. We've all heard stories about inheritances being wasted or used frivolously.

> **Creative Trust Planning:** I once read of a man who was a highly successful business owner. His intention was to split his vast wealth among his many grandchildren upon his death. But he was concerned that his grandchildren might behave as wastrels, neglecting college education, ambition and character in knowing they could safely rely on grandpa's riches to coast through life.
>
> His solution was simple. He directed all the money to a trust with just three instructions for the trustee: the first was that all assets were to be split equally between the grandchildren. The second was that each distribution was to be made only when a grandchild reached the age of 30, in hopes that the grandchild would be beyond the immaturity that marks early adulthood. But the third part was the real kicker. It stipulated that for a grandchild to earn their share, they must be earning the inflation-adjusted equivalent of $100,000 per year in the career path of their choosing.
>
> This final clause ensured that any prodigal grandchild would forfeit their inheritance. To receive their share, they would need to have already achieved success through their own efforts! Otherwise, the trustee was directed to donate that grandchild's money to charity. Talk about incentive!
>
> The grandfather in our story recognized that an inheritance could be a blessing as much as it could be a curse. A properly considered and structured trust can protect the people you care about just as much as it can protect the money and assets.

I'm of the opinion that nearly everyone can benefit from a trust for the avoidance of probate alone. But others will find additional value in the myriad ways that trusts can be customized to suit your family's needs and goals.

Pour-Over Will

Some visitors to our office beam with pride when they report that they've already completed an estate plan, and set up a trust to protect their beneficiaries and avoid probate. My response is always the same, "Great job setting up a trust! *What's in it?*" Half the time, I'm met with a blank stare in return.

A trust doesn't provide any protection for your assets unless it's *funded*. Many people falsely assume that their trust is some sort of asset vacuum cleaner that sucks up and protects all your assets just by its very existence. Not true!

A trust is a legal container. Anything inside the container is protected. But anything outside of it is not. You must register assets into the trust or designate the trust as a beneficiary for the assets to be afforded any protection.

Not all assets are easily transferred to a trust for a variety of reasons. That's why we suggest pairing a living trust with a pour-over will. This document specifies that all assets not already in trust will be directed there immediately upon your death. It's effectively a safety measure that attempts to make sure no assets escape inclusion in the trust. However, like all wills a pour-over is subject to probate so its use should be limited to a fail-safe measure rather than a catchall.

Health Care Proxy and Living Will

Estate planning entails more than making arrangements for the transfer of assets to beneficiaries. You need to exercise as much care in providing legal protections for yourself while alive.

Consider the case of Terri Schiavo, the Florida woman who suffered severe brain damage following cardiac arrest. After months of examination, doctors officially diagnosed her as being in a persistent vegetative state without any visible signs of improvement. Subsequently, Ms. Schiavo endured seven years of legal tug-of-war waged between her husband, who insisted Terri would not want to persist in such condition and her parents, who countered that their daughter should be given every opportunity to recover. Their battle eventually involved state and federal courts, Florida's governor and state legislature, the U.S. Congress, the Supreme Court and even the president himself!

The case cost millions of dollars in medical and legal fees and incredible suffering for the family on both sides. Sadly, we'll never know what Terri endured along that stretch. But we do know that almost all the hullabaloo could have been avoided had Terri *documented* her wishes.

Everyone should consider electing a health care proxy—a person designated with legal documentation to make medical decisions on your behalf if you are incapable of doing so yourself. Your proxy can exercise control over the scope and direction of any potential medical treatment according to their discretion, so this should be a person you trust and have informed of your wishes. This election serves to avoid unnecessary emotional turmoil within a family as well as protect your own integrity.

If you'd prefer not to entrust the direction of your health care to another person, there is a viable alternative. A living will outlines specific treatments you want *or do not want* to receive in the event you're unable to communicate, such as resuscitation, artificial nutrition, hydration and mechanical ventilation.

Durable Financial Power of Attorney

Another vital element of the Five Essentials is the durable financial power of attorney. Similar in many ways to the health care proxy, it appoints an individual to make financial decisions on your behalf if you are incapacitated.

I once heard an attorney tell a distressing story. For years, she had encouraged her aunt and uncle to draft an estate plan. However, the effort was postponed. Sadly, the uncle suffered an unexpected and devastating stroke that left him in a coma.

His wife wanted to spare no expense in giving him a chance to make a full recovery. After their health insurance reached its lifetime limit, she began calling banks, mutual fund companies and other financial institutions to get access to additional money. Unfortunately, since her husband had been both primary breadwinner and overseer of their finances, almost all the accounts were in his name. Because she was not an account owner and without power of attorney, she was unable to access the funds!

There *is* a remedial process for this, known as a living probate. But it can be every bit as burdensome, complicated, time consuming and expensive as the other probate process. The aunt eventually got access to the funds, but not without great pain, delay and expense. All of this could have been avoided by including a durable financial power of attorney in their estate plan.

Homestead Exemption

Homestead exemptions have existed in the U.S. since the 18th century. They protect the value of the principal residence from creditors, property taxes or other financial hardships commonly associated with bankruptcy or the death of a spouse. Every state with the exceptions of Delaware, New Jersey, Pennsylvania and Rhode Island offer some form of exemption. But the protection is not necessarily automatic and, depending on your state of domicile, you may be required to file with the state or county to claim your exemption.

The homestead exemption effectively serves as state-provided insurance to protect a limited amount of the value of your home for both living and decedent purposes. Round out your Five Essentials by discovering if additional work is needed to include the homestead exemption in your estate plan. A call to your local registry of deeds is a good place to start if you cannot find relevant information concerning your state's exemption protections or registration process online. Be sure to carefully record the protection benefits, as well as the limitations, so your beneficiaries can stay organized.

Advanced Planning

The Five Essentials are a great starting point for maximizing the protection of your assets at relatively low cost and little complexity. Some people may want to explore advanced estate planning techniques to take tax avoidance or Medicaid eligibility to the next level.

Estate Tax Planning — Federal estate tax used to be a much bigger problem until the government raised the estate tax exemption to $5 million in 2012. Due to inflation indexing, you can leave up to $5.49 million to your beneficiaries, exempt of all federal estate and gift taxes in 2017. A couple can leave up to $10.98 million! Keep in mind that state estate taxes may apply, depending on where you live and where your physical assets are located.

While most Americans won't have to worry about estate taxes, those with estates exceeding the exempted limits will pay a *40 percent tax* on the excess. If you find yourself in this category, pay attention to what follows!

First, if you're married, note that the full $10.98 million exemption is not automatic. For the estate to be fully sheltered, you must claim the $5.49 million exemption on the estate tax return of the first spouse to die *even though no tax is due when transferring assets between spouses.* This maneuver is called *portability,* and those who overlook it may miss out on invaluable protection.

Gifting — You can also decrease the value of your taxable estate by giving away money during your lifetime. You're allowed to gift up to $14,000 per year to anyone of your choosing without affecting your estate exemption limits. A married couple can give up to $28,000 per person per year. This is known as the annual exclusion and can go a long way in funding college for grandchildren or other purposes. Just be sure to consult your tax advisor concerning tax liabilities for which your intended recipients may be responsible.

Interested in giving away more? Gifts to charity can be made without any limitations. There's also no restriction on paying for the medical expenses for whomever you'd like to cover, provided that the payments are made directly to the service provider.

Irrevocable Trusts

Medicaid Planning — It's a common sentiment: "I'd rather the money go to the kids than the medical system!" But this is easier said than done. As explored in the chapter on health care, *someone* has to pay the bill. Once Medicare benefits cease, the payor of last resort is Medicaid. But you only become eligible for Medicaid after spending assets down to an impoverished state.

You can advance toward Medicaid eligibility by removing assets from your name and control with an *irrevocable* trust. Unlike its revocable cousin, the irrevocable trust cannot be changed once established and you can only serve as a grantor, never a trustee. This means you can add assets to the trust, but a third party must be put in control of the assets and trust administration. Beneficiary elections and the conditions under which assets are to be distributed are considered permanent and cannot be revoked unless consented to by the beneficiaries and trustees.

Assets within an irrevocable trust are effectively inaccessible to you except under extremely limited circumstances. The upside is that the assets placed in this trust effectively become invisible to the Medicaid system. Hence, you can become Medicaid eligible without having to spend down all your assets! This strategy makes it possible to be certain that some of your assets are protected and will be passed to the beneficiaries of your choice.

However, it's not unlike giving the money away while living. By funding an irrevocable trust, you are forfeiting control of the assets, including the right to sell, manage, invest or spend them. Additionally, the assets must have been placed in trust *five years* in advance of appealing for Medicaid assistance. Otherwise, the assets are counted against Medicaid eligibility and penalties may apply.

Given these restrictions, the use of irrevocable trusts for Medicaid planning is not very common. Few people are comfortable forfeiting control and access to their assets regardless of the potential benefits. Still, the irrevocable trust has other ways of becoming a tremendously powerful estate-planning tool:

ILIT — One way to transfer wealth to future generations is through life insurance. Most people are familiar with the fact that life insurance proceeds are not subject to income tax. Unfortunately, life insurance proceeds are not exempt from estate tax. However, this can be circumvented by placing your life insurance policy in an irrevocable life insurance trust (ILIT). High net worth individuals can transfer large sums of wealth combining an ILIT with annual gifting.

Large Asset Transfers — Another example of strategic irrevocable trust application entails using your $5.49 million exemption today while *living*. If you have an asset intended for the next generation that may be worth significantly more in the future, it might be beneficial to transfer the asset *now* by utilizing the exemption sooner rather than later.

This can be an ideal strategy for rental or commercial real estate property owners. These properties might only be worth a modest amount now, but in 10, 20 or 30 years they could easily be worth many millions. If the intention is to keep the property in the family, you could consider giving away the properties tax-free using your lifetime exemption today. This allows the property value to accumulate without risk of exposure to estate taxes when the properties are worth considerably more. Assets that may warrant this kind of transfer include businesses, valuable heirlooms or concentrated investment positions. Trusts make an excellent vehicle for these transfers.

For high net worth individuals with estates worth more than $5 million, irrevocable trusts are sometimes viewed as a necessity to help protect some or all the estate. But for those with more modest holdings, these trusts should only be used selectively and with great care, given the forfeiture of flexibility.

Special Needs Trusts — We routinely meet with people who have children or other family members in their care that are receiving some level of state benefits. Caution must be exercised in transferring assets to these individuals since any gifts or inheritance may make them ineligible for aid. If you have concerns in this area be sure to bring this to the attention of your attorney and advisor.

Expect Changes — As of this writing, the Trump administration is proposing that the estate tax be eliminated. Regardless of whether it passes, it's important to note that the legal winds can shift from one political administration to the next. We advise that you have your estate plan reviewed every two to four years to make sure it remains compliant with current law. Not all law firms will keep you posted automatically, so be sure to choose your legal team wisely.

A Word on Cost

Attorneys charge wildly different rates for estate planning and document preparation. A basic will typically costs a few hundred dollars while a standalone trust goes for a thousand or two. Estate planning packages that include all Five Essentials will be more, as will situations with more complicated considerations.

I've seen attorneys charge $10,000 or more for package services. That's too much, in my opinion. Paying more than $5,000 is reasonable only when a situation is complicated. Do you own property in more than one state? Do you have children from multiple marriages? Do you have a large or demanding set of goals and wishes? If these or other considerations apply to your circumstances, then you may need the Rolls Royce of estate plans. For most of us, shopping for a more budget-friendly approach will be fine.

Arcadia Financial Group has arranged with many local attorneys to help our clients prepare the Five Essentials at substantially discounted rates in the $2,000–$3,000 range as of this writing. We'd be happy to make a referral if appropriate.

ON-TRACK ESTATE PLANNING FOCUS

Are you certain that your assets will avoid probate? Does your plan protect your family as much as it protects your assets? Is your plan documented and accessible to your close family members in the case of emergency?

Call us today to review your estate plan (888) ARCADIA, or visit us online at www.railsofsteel.com.

CHAPTER TEN

Your Ticket to Retirement

e call our holistic planning process **Your Ticket to Retirement**. Like the steam engineers of old, we endeavor to place retirement on a steady course, at the time of your choice and to the destination of your choosing. Using our knowledge of the past, but being mindful of the challenges of tomorrow, we help our clients navigate through financial tools and strategies to customize retirement plans that provide dependable income for life.

No stone goes unturned. We'll help you explore income strategies, health care solutions and methods to defend yourself against taxes and inflation. We also carefully coordinate our planning process with prudent legal strategies to help you protect your assets for the next generation.

Best of all, because we're independent, we're not limited to the product line or agenda of some parent company. As a fiduciary firm, we work exclusively to serve the unique interests of each client. It's financial planning done the way it should be.

Is it time we had a chat?

Request a Consultation:

Call:

(603) 681-9190 or (888) ARCADIA

Email:

retire@arcadiafg.com

Visit:

www.railsofsteel.com

ABOUT THE AUTHOR

Michael R. Panico, CFP®, has been helping clients plan for retirement for over 15 years. Prior to founding Arcadia Financial Group, Mike served as an advisor with Equity Services, Inc. and Ameriprise Financial.

Mike holds a Bachelor of Science degree in Finance from Babson College and achieved the CERTIFIED FINANCIAL PLANNER™

designation in 2008. The CFP® designation is granted only to advisors who have completed rigorous examination demonstrating their ability to professionally deliver on many traditional planning aspects including: insurance planning and risk management, employee benefits planning, investment planning, income tax planning, retirement planning and estate planning. CFP® professionals are vetted to uphold the highest standards of education, experience and ethics.

Mike is also a member of the The Million Dollar Round Table's Top of the Table, a career milestone.

Mike was born and raised in Dedham, Massachusetts, but now resides in New Hampshire with his wife and two sons. He holds a resident license for life, accident and health insurance in the state of New Hampshire. Insurance services may also be offered in other states.

Investment advisory services are offered through Arcadia Wealth Management, LLC, a Registered Investment Adviser. Insurance products and services are offered and sold through Arcadia Financial Group, LLC and individually licensed and appointed insurance agents. Arcadia Financial Group, LLC and Arcadia Wealth Management, LLC are affiliated but separate entities.

Investing involves risk, including the loss of principal. No investment strategy can guarantee a profit or protect against loss in periods of declining values. Any references to protection benefits or lifetime income generally refer to fixed insurance products, never securities or investment products. Insurance and annuity product guarantees are backed by the financial strength and claims-paying ability of the issuing insurance company.

We are not permitted to offer and no statement made in this book shall constitute tax or legal advice. You should talk to a qualified professional before making any decisions about your personal situation.

94033927R00103

Made in the USA
Lexington, KY
23 July 2018